THE BOFFINS BAFFLED

<u>What chemistry, we are often asked</u>, takes place in the succulent bosom of the sherry casks where The Macallan lies slumbering for a decade (at least) before it is allowed out to meet the bottle?

The fact is, we do not know.

It is a <u>matter of history</u>, of course, that someone in the last century discovered that whisky ages best in oaken casks which have previously contained sherry (and that today The Macallan is the <u>last malt whisky</u> exclusively to be so matured).

And it is a <u>matter of fact</u> that in goes the translucent stripling spirit. And out comes amber-gold nectar positively <u>billowing</u> with flavour.

But let us take our cue from a party of scientists whom we once invited to explore the matter. '*Magic!*' they exclaimed, swigging their drams in a most unboffinly manner. 'But magic is merely undiscovered science and we'd like to take some home <u>for further investigation</u>.'

To join our small (but devoted) band of merry malt sippers, please call 1-800-428-9810.

THE MACALLAN. THE MALT.

THE MACALLAN® Scotch Whisky. 43% alc./vol. Sole U.S. importer Rémy Amerique, Inc., New York, N.Y. © 1998 Macallan-Glenlivet P.L.C.

ELAINE

LOVES

THE PARIS REVIEW

ELAINE'S
1703 SECOND AVE
NEW YORK CITY

reservations: 534-8103/8114

The Paris Review

Founded in 1953.
Publisher Drue Heinz
Editors
George Plimpton, Peter Matthiessen, Donald Hall, Robert Silvers, Blair Fuller, Maxine Groffsky, Jeanne McCulloch, James Linville

Managing Editor	Daniel Kunitz
Editor at Large	Elizabeth Gaffney
Senior Editor	Brigid Hughes
Associate Editors	Stephen Clark, Eliza Griswold Allen
Assistant Editor	Fiona Maazel
Poetry Editor	Richard Howard
Art Editor	Joan Krawczyk
London Editor Shusha Guppy	**Paris Editor** Harry Mathews
Business Manager Lillian von Nickern	**Treasurer** Marjorie Kalman
Design Consultant	Chip Kidd
Editorial Assistants	Dana Goodyear, Lauren Neefe

Readers
Charles Buice, Scott Conklin, Jon Curley, Gates Hinds, James Lavino, James Zug

Special Consultants
Anthony Haden-Guest, Noah Harlan, W. Gardner Knight, Robert Phillips, Ben Sonnenberg, Remar Sutton

Advisory Editors
Nelson Aldrich, Andy Bellin, Lawrence M. Bensky, Patrick Bowles, Christopher Cerf, Jonathan Dee, Timothy Dickinson, Joan Dillon, Beth Drenning, David Evanier, Anne Fulenwider, Rowan Gaither, David Gimbel, Francine du Plessix Gray, Lindy Guinness, Fayette Hickox, Ben Howe, Susannah Hunnewell, Ben Johnson, Gia Kourlas, Mary B. Lumet, Larissa MacFarquhar, Molly McKaughan, Jonathan Miller, Ron Padgett, Maggie Paley, John Phillips, Kevin Richardson, David Robbins, Philip Roth, Elissa Schappell, Frederick Seidel, Mona Simpson, Max Steele, William Styron, Tim Sultan, Hallie Gay Walden, Christopher Walker, Antonio Weiss

Contributing Editors
Agha Shahid Ali, Robert Antoni, Kip Azzoni, Sara Barrett, Helen Bartlett, Robert Becker, Adam Begley, Magda Bogin, Chris Calhoun, Morgan Entrekin, Robert Faggen, Jill Fox, Jamey Gambrell, John Glusman, Edward Hirsch, Gerald Howard, Tom Jenks, Barbara Jones, Fran Kiernan, Mary Maguire, Lucas Matthiessen, Dan Max, Joanie McDonnell, Molly McGrann, David Michaelis, Elise Paschen, Allen Peacock, William Plummer, Charles Russell, Michael Sagalyn, David Salle, Elisabeth Sifton, Ileene Smith, Rose Styron, William Wadsworth, Julia Myer Ward, John Zinsser

Poetry Editors
Donald Hall (1953–1961), X.J. Kennedy (1962–1964), Thomas Clark (1964–1973), Michael Benedikt (1974–1978), Jonathan Galassi (1978–1988), Patricia Storace (1988–1992)

Art Editors
William Pène du Bois (1953–1960), Paris Editors (1961–1974), Alexandra Anderson (1974–1978), Richard Marshall (1978–1993)

Founding Publisher   Sadruddin Aga Khan

Former Publishers
Bernard F. Conners, Ron Dante, Deborah S. Pease

Founding Editors
Peter Matthiessen, Harold L. Humes, George Plimpton, William Pène du Bois, Thomas H. Guinzburg, John Train

The Paris Review is published quarterly by The Paris Review, Inc. Vol. 40, No. 148, Fall 1998. Business Office: 45-39 171st Place, Flushing, New York 11358 (ISSN #0031-2037). Paris Office: Harry Mathews, 67 rue de Grenelle, Paris 75007 France. London Office: Shusha Guppy, 8 Shawfield St., London, SW3. US distributors: Random House, Inc. 1(800)733-3000. Typeset and printed in USA by Capital City Press, Montpelier, VT. Price for single issue in USA: $10.00. $14.00 in Canada. Post-paid subscription for four issues $34.00, lifetime subscription $1000. Postal surcharge of $10.00 per four issues outside USA (excluding life subscriptions). Subscription card is bound within magazine. Please give six weeks notice of change of address using subscription card. While The Paris Review welcomes the submission of unsolicited manuscripts, it cannot accept responsibility for their loss or delay, or engage in related correspondence. Manuscripts will not be returned or responded to unless accompanied by self-addressed, stamped envelope. Fiction manuscripts should be submitted to George Plimpton, poetry to Richard Howard, The Paris Review, 541 East 72nd Street, New York, N.Y. 10021. Charter member of the Council of Literary Magazines and Presses. This publication is made possible, in part, with public funds from the New York State Council on the Arts and the National Endowment for the Arts. Periodicals postage paid at Flushing, New York, and at additional mailing offices. **Postmaster:** Please send address changes to 45-39 171st Place, Flushing, N.Y. 11358.

NOON

EDITED BY DIANE WILLIAMS

NEW   PLEASE SEND FICTION

1369 MADISON AVENUE   SUITE 298   NEW YORK   NEW YORK   10128

The last poems from
"The wisest poet of his generation."*

WILLIAM MATTHEWS

After
ALL
LAST POEMS

Photo: Ted Rosenberg

"An extraordinarily important American poet."—Gerald Stern

*Peter Stitt, *Georgia Review*

 At bookstores everywhere
HOUGHTON MIFFLIN *Independent publishers since 1832*

THE CONTEST CONSULTANT
WRITE*Time* 1998 ✓

Gives you time to write!
Thousands of updates for 1998
Hundreds of New Contests

- Software designed by a writer for writers
- Lists over 2,000 contests, fellowships, scholarships, grants and awards
- Searches under categories or deadlines
- Tracks award submissions and queries
- Add or delete to create your own database

14 CATEGORIES
Short Story
Novel
Poetry
Drama
Gay/Lesbian
Journalism
Screen/Teleplays
Residency
Nonfiction/
Scholarly
Commercial
Children's Lit
Translation
Religion
Women

💾 **$80** WINDOWS/MAC

WRITE*Suite*
PURCHASE BOTH FOR ONLY
💾💾 **$100**

THE MANUSCRIPT MANAGER
WRITE*Trak*

**A Writer writes,
WriteTrak does the rest!**

WriteTrak tracks:
- SUBMISSIONS by Date, Manuscript Title, Publisher, Subject
- PUBLISHERS by Name, Submission Date, Manuscript Title
- MANUSCRIPTS by Title, Submission Date, Publisher
- EXPENSES by Date, Manuscript

UPDATES & PRINTS
Expense Reports
Letters
Resumes
CV
Manuscripts
Publish & Submission History

💾 **$50** WINDOWS/MAC

Visa/MC Accepted

1-800-891-0962

Grossman Development Company
P.O. Box 85732, Seattle, WA 98145-1732
e-mail: gdc@earthlink.net http://www.writetime.com

YMCA National Writer's Voice
A Network of Literary Arts Centers at YMCAs

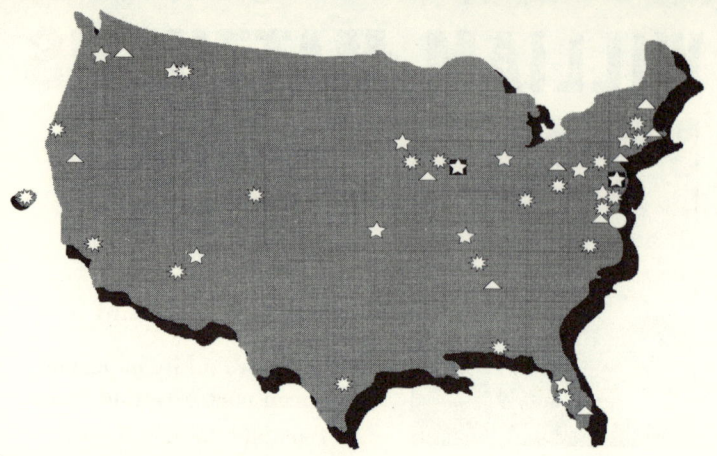

☆ **Core Centers**: *Billings, MT • Scottsdale, AZ • Fairfield, CT • Chicago, IL • Lexington, KY • Minneapolis, MN • Chesterfield, MO • Bay Shore, NY • New York, NY • Silver Bay, NY • Detroit, MI • Tampa, FL*

△ **New Centers**: *Huntington, NY • Atlanta, GA • Charlottesville, VA • Providence, RI • Miami, FL • Quincy, IL • Wethersfield, CT • Gardena, CA • Manchester, NH • Everett, WA*

◯ **Armed Services Center**: *Springfield, VA •*

☆ **Program Schools**: *Tempe, AZ • Mobile, AL • Pawling, NY • Des Moines, IA • Houston, TX • Denver, CO • San Francisco, CA • Tampa, FL • Columbus, OH • Springfield, MA • Baltimore, MD • Long Beach, CA • Tacoma, WA • West Chester, PA • Rockford, IL • Nashville, TN • Billings, MT • Honolulu, HI • Boston, MA • Black Mountain, NC • Rochester, NY (Program Schools offer year-round training in literary arts program development to YMCA staff.)*

■ YMCA National Writer's Voice Office • YMCA of the USA National Office

*International Centers in development: *France, Israel, Italy and South Africa*

YMCA Writer's Voice centers meet the particular needs of their communities through public readings, workshops, writing camps for youth, magazine publishing, in-school residencies, and other literary arts activities while offering national programs such as the National Readings Tour, the National Readings Network, The Writers Community Writer-in-Residence Program, and the Body-in-Question Reading & Discussion Program. Centers also participate in national conferences, funding initiatives, and program sharing.

Contact your local YMCA or the YMCA National Writer's Voice Office
5 West 63rd Street • New York, NY 10023 • 212.875.4261

A program of the YMCA of the USA, funded by the YMCA, Lila Wallace-Reader's Digest Fund, National Endowment for the Arts, National Endowment for the Humanities, The William Bingham Foundation, and the Lannan Foundation, as well as many regional, state, and local organizations.

NEW THIS FALL

THE VIEW FROM POMPEY'S HEAD
HAMILTON BASSO

"Basso's most impressive book.... A long, mildly ironic, and deliberately discursive work, it weaves two of his favorite subjects, the subtle social distinctions of a small southern city and the subtle questions of reputation and standing in New York literary and publishing circles."—*Saturday Review*

$16.95 paper

TAKE ME BACK
RICHARD BAUSCH

"Bausch [takes] us into the minds of his three characters for an honest exploration of the binding and dissolving tensions in modern family life."—*Library Journal*

"Be aware of Bausch as a writer . . . who has complete control of his craft."—*Publishers Weekly*

$15.95 paper

THE INKLING
FRED CHAPPELL

"A dark and terrifying tale, told with artistic skill and considerable insight into the tortured minds of these lonely characters."—*Chicago Daily News*

"His story holds our attention as might the glittering eye of a coiled snake."—*Southern Observer*

$12.95 paper

BOBBY REX'S GREATEST HIT
MARIANNE GINGHER

"Gingher has captured, with writing that is southern poetry, the raw-nerved state of being that was endured by teen-age girls of the fifties and early sixties."
—*Washington Post*

"By turns hilarious, wry . . . meditative and almost rhapsodically lyrical."—*New York Times Book Review*

$14.95 paper

*V*OICES OF THE *S*OUTH
CELEBRATING THE BEST IN SOUTHERN WRITING

LOUISIANA STATE ♀ UNIVERSITY PRESS
P.O. Box 25053 · Baton Rouge 70894-5053 · 800-861-3477

REYNOLDS PRICE

LEARNING A TRADE
A Craftsman's Notebooks, 1955–1997

From Reynolds Price, much acclaimed author of award-winning novels, plays, poems, stories, and essays, comes a work that is unique among contemporary writers of American literature. For more than forty years, Price has kept a working journal of his writing life. Now published for the first time, *Learning a Trade* provides a revealing window into this writer's creative process and craftsman's sensibilities.

"Reynolds Price's life, while as unique as his thumbprint, turns out here to be a strikingly general anatomy of virtually every good writer's artistic development from childhood on. I would not have thought that generalizations about growth in such a complex profession were plausible—until this meticulous dissection was shown to me."—*Kurt Vonnegut*

624 pages, cloth $34.95

DUKE UNIVERSITY PRESS
Available at bookstores or toll-free 1-888-651-0122

RADICAL SHADOWS

CONJUNCTIONS:31

Edited by Bradford Morrow and Peter Constantine

A landmark collection of previously unpublished and untranslated work by 19th and 20th century masters, including:

Anton Chekhov

Djuna Barnes

Fyodor Dostoyevsky

Thomas Bernhard

Vaslav Nijinsky

Yasunari Kawabata

Elizabeth Bishop

Marcel Proust

Anna Akhmatova

Truman Capote

... and work by 15 other major writers.

Available now in quality bookshops.
Or, order online at www.Conjunctions.com.

For more information, contact:

Conjunctions
Bard College
Annandale-on-Hudson, NY 12504
(914) 758-1539

Published by Bard College

The Paris Review

Editorial Office:
541 East 72 Street
New York, New York 10021
HTTP://www.parisreview.com

Business & Circulation:
45-39 171 Place
Flushing, New York 11358

Distributed by Random House
201 East 50 Street
New York, N.Y. 10022
(800) 733-3000

Table of contents illustration by Karen Kilimnik, *Sugar*, crayon and pastel on paper, 40″ × 26″, 1994.
Frontispiece by William Pène du Bois.

Number 148

Interviews
V.S. Naipaul	*The Art of Fiction CLIV*	38
Mark Strand	*The Art of Poetry LXXVII*	146

Fiction
Louis de Bernières	*Our Lady of Beauty*	67
A.L. Kennedy	*Indelible Acts*	179
Norman Lock	*A Treatise on Desire*	223
J. David Stevens	*The Sniper's Story*	129
Joy Williams	*Substance*	14

Features
Simon Armitage	*Jerusalem*	106
Kurt Vonnegut	*L'histoire du soldat*	188

Art
Alan Loehle	*Six Dogs*	99
Mark Strand	*Island Monotype*	cover

Poetry
Neil Azevedo	*Three Poems*	212
Diann Blakely	*The Dolls*	222
Scott Coffel	*Andrei and Natasha*	145
Alfred Corn	*Who, What, Where, When, Why?*	36
Rachel Hadas	*Searching the Scriptures*	205
Anthony Hecht	*Le Jet d'Eau*	131
Melanie Hope	*Sixth Grade*	137
Sue Kwock Kim	*Two Poems*	141
Wayne Koestenbaum	*Splinters*	92
Daniel Kunitz	*Two Poems*	28
Richard Lamb	*Three Poems*	207
Rachel Loden	*Two Poems*	34
Stephen McLeod	*Two Poems*	138
John McKernan	*Room Service*	85
Susan Mitchell	*Autobiography*	96
Nick Norwood	*A Palace for the Heart*	220
Eric Ormsby	*Two Poems*	30
Kathleen Peirce	*Four Poems*	82
Carl Phillips	*Of That City, the Heart*	80
Bin Ramke	*A Great Noise the World Makes*	133
Stephen Sandy	*Five Poems*	86
Daniel Tobin	*Floor Scrapers*	37
Kevin Young	*Homage to Phillis Wheatley*	32

Notes on Contributors	234

Substance

Joy Williams

Walter got the silk pajamas clearly worn. Dianne got the candlesticks. Tim got the two lilac bushes, one French purple, one white—an alarming gift, lilacs being so evocative of the depth and dumbness of death's kingdom, they made Tim cry. They were large and had to be removed with a backhoe, which did not please the landlord, who didn't get anything, although he didn't have to return the last month's rent deposit either. Lucretia got the manhattan glasses. They were delicate, with a scroll of flowers etched just beneath the rim. There were four of them. Andrew got the wristwatch. Betsy got the barbells. Jack got a fairly useless silver bowl. Angus got the photo basket, Louise got the dog.

Louise would have preferred anything to the dog, right down to the barbells. Or nothing would have pleased her even more. It was believed that the animal had been witness to the suicide. He might possibly have been in the kitchen eating his chow or napping on the porch but it was more likely that he'd been in the bedroom, taking in the entire performance.

He was a quiet, medium-sized dog. He wasn't one of those dogs who would have sounded the alarm. He wasn't one of those dogs who would have attempted to prevent the removal of the body from the house.

Louise took the dog immediately to a kennel, where she boarded it. She couldn't imagine why she, of all people, had been given the dog. But in the note Elliot left he had clearly stated, *And to Louise my dog, Broom.* The worst of it was that none of them remembered Elliot having a dog. They had never seen the dog before. Suddenly there was a dog in the picture.

"He said he was thinking of getting a dog sometime," Jack said.

"But wouldn't he have said, 'I got a dog . . .' He never said that," Dianne said.

"He must have just gotten it. Maybe he got it the day before. Or even that morning, maybe," Angus said.

This alarmed Louise.

"I'm sure he never thought you'd keep it," Lucretia said.

This alarmed her even more.

"Oh, I don't know!" Lucretia said. "I just wanted to make you feel better."

Louise saw her friends practically constantly but sometimes she liked to be alone. One evening she was sitting alone in a bar, worrying about the money it was costing to board the dog who had been at the kennel now for a week and a half. The dog weighed under thirty-five pounds but that still meant eleven dollars a day. If he had weighed between fifty and seventy-five it would have been fourteen dollars and after that it was even worse, it went up again even.

In the bar was a long tank, which served as a wall separating the restaurant beyond. Louise had never been in this place before and would not select it again. She didn't like to look at the fish, one of which was trailing a cloud of mucus behind it. In the restaurant beyond the fish, she saw an older man deep in conversation with a party or parties outside her vision. He was a large square-faced man in a green plaid shirt, with moist, closely cut hair and a Band-Aid high up on his temple. A line of blood extended several inches down from the Band-Aid. Louise became engrossed in watching the man, who was chatting and smiling and sawing away at his steak or whatever it was. But she looked away for a moment and when she looked back the blood was gone. He must have wiped it away with a napkin, perhaps dipped in his water glass. Someone in the party he was with loved him and told him about the blood, was Louise's first thought, then she thought that it had certainly taken them long enough to mention it.

The next morning she went to the kennel. A girl brought the dog out. It had yellowish, wavy fur.

"Is that the right one?" Louise asked. The girl looked at her expressionlessly and cracked her gum. "It's really not mine," Louise explained, "it belongs to a friend."

The dog crouched miserably on the floor in the backseat of Louise's car. It didn't even lie down.

"You're going to get sick down there," Louise said. The dog was clearly not used to riding in cars. It seemed to have no sense of the happiness that could bring.

A week passed and she discerned no habits. The dog didn't seem morose, merely withdrawn. She began calling it Broom with a certain amount of reluctance. It seemed that by calling it Broom, she was agreeing to something that she'd prefer not to.

Every week there would be a party at one of their houses. It wasn't Louise's turn right yet. She went over to Jack's and everyone was already there. Everyone was drinking gimlets and looking at a rat Jack had caught beneath the sink on a glue trap.

"I'm not going to use these things again," Jack said. "They're depressing."

"I use them," Walter said, "but I never get any rats."

"You're not putting them in the right place," Jack said.

The rat watched them in a sort of theatrical way. One of

the twins, Wilbur, got up and opened a window. He picked up the glue trap by its edge and sailed it into the street to fall amidst the passing traffic.

"I usually take it down to the dumpster," Jack said.

Wilbur and his twin Daisy were the only ones who said they remembered Broom. They said that he hadn't eaten from a bowl but off a Columbia University dinner plate. But Wilbur and Daisy in their far-out nods could picture anything. They spent most of their time lovingly shooting one another up. They had not been mentioned in the note as gift recipients although of course they didn't care. They insisted that matters would not have taken such a dreary turn had they been able to introduce Elliot to the great Heroisch, the potent, powerful, large and appealing Heroisch. The twins were so innocent they got on everyone's nerves. They loved throwing up on junk. A joy develops, they'd say, a real joy. It's not like throwing up at all.

They all had their big quietly rotting houses, even the twins. Rent was cheap. Louise had a solarium in hers, although it leaked badly. To the rear of the house, there was an overgrown yard with a birdhouse nailed to each tree. Some trees had more than one. The previous tenant must have been demented, Louise thought, why would birds want to live like that?

At Jack's they drank, but lightly, except for Dianne, who was drinking far too much recently. She'd said, "I began to wonder if it was worthwhile to undertake what I was doing at the moment. Pick a moment, any moment. I began to wonder. If I had only today and not tomorrow, would it be worthwhile to undertake what I was doing at the moment? I addressed myself to that very worthwhile question and I had to admit, well, no." But no one tried to interfere with Dianne. They were getting over the death of their friend Elliot, each in his and her own way, was the understanding.

"It takes four full seasons to get over a death," Angus said.
"Spring and summer, winter and fall."
"Fall and winter," Andrew said.

Everyone was a little annoyed with Angus because he had taken all the photos out of the flat woven basket where Elliot had always kept them and arranged them in albums, apparently ordered by years or occasions. This pleased no one. It wasn't the same. The effect was different. Everything had looked like a gala before. Now none of it looked like a gala.

Wilbur said, "We've been reading Pablo Neruda, and Daisy came across the line *Death also goes through the world dressed like a broom.*"

"I did," Daisy said.

"Dressed?" Louise said. "What do you mean 'dressed'?"

"It's a bad translation probably," Betsy said.

"Neruda is a giant among pygmies," Wilbur said. "You can't argue with Neruda, his mind was impeccable."

"Dressed it was," Daisy insisted.

"Couldn't you keep your mouths shut about this?" Dianne said to the twins.

They began talking about the things Elliot had given them. They could not understand what he had been attempting to say. All his other things had been trucked away and stored. A brother was supposed to come for them. But he was sick or lived in Turkey or some goddamned place, who cared . . . He hadn't shown up yet in any case.

More than a month passed. Louise was working at a florist's shop and sometimes at an automobile glass-tinting establishment, cutting and ironing on the darkest film allowable by law, which was 20 percent, less than most people wanted but all they were going to get. Her own car had a confetti sparkle on the rear glass. It was like a little burst of fireworks going off in the darkness of her glass. She liked the florist's. She liked working there, at the long cutting table, wearing an apricot-colored smock, among the unnatural blooms. A woman came in one day, just before closing. She wanted to send a dozen roses to a young veterinarian assistant.

"My dog bit her when she tried to lift him for an X ray," the woman said. "I'm so embarrassed."

Louise had never been interested in the reasons people bought flowers. "I don't like dogs," Louise said.

"Really?" the woman said. "I don't know where I'd be without my Buckie."

"You wouldn't be in here buying these roses," Louise said.

Another season insinuated itself. It was Tim's turn to give a party, but things were not going well with Tim. The lilacs had not survived transplanting. They would never come back. Tim had done his best but his best wasn't good enough. He had also had an unhappy experience with a pair of swans. He had been following their fortunes ever since he had witnessed them mating in a marsh beside the highway. "They twined their necks like heraldry afterwards," he said. "Heraldry." But the male, after weeks of guarding the nest, disappeared and a week later, the female vanished. Tim had watched them so arduously, and suddenly they were gone. He was sure someone had murdered them, poisoned them. "Remember the *Lied* about the swan?" he asked.

"Leda and the swan?" Angus volunteered.

"The German song," Tim said impatiently. "The *Lied*," he said, upset.

It was about a swan who so loved a hunter by the marsh that she became a woman and married him and had three children. Then one night the king of the swans called to her to come back, or else he would die, so slowly she turned into a swan again, and slowly she opened her wide, white wings, and left her husband and her children . . .

"Her wide, white wings," Tim said, his eyes open, weeping. But no one knew the *Lied*. No one could help Tim with remembering the *Lied* precisely.

Lucretia gave a party out of turn. Everyone came but Dianne and Tim. Walter asked Louise about the dog.

"Old Broom," Louise answered. "Poor Broom." The dog was not demanding, it was modest in its requirements, although it drank a lot of water; it liked its water. It could square itself off like a package in a chair, it could actually resemble a package. That was about it. Everyone half-expected that Broom would have disappeared by now, *run away*.

"Listen," Lucretia said. "I'll tell you. One of those glasses

I was given got a little chip on the rim and I found myself going to a jeweler's and getting an estimate for filing it down. It cost seventy-five dollars and I paid half of that and I left it there. I'm not picking it up. I didn't even give them the right telephone number. I decided enough's enough."

Walter confessed that he had thrown away the silk pajamas immediately, without a modicum of ceremony.

"None of it makes a bit of sense," Betsy said. "What would I want with barbells? I took those barbells down to the park and left them by the softball field. You're a saint, Louise. I could see you maybe not wanting to take it to the pound but I always thought—she's going to take it to a no-kill facility."

"What do you mean?" Louise asked.

"A no-kill facility. Isn't that self-explanatory?"

"Well no," Louise said, "not really. I mean it doesn't sound all that great somehow."

"Most places keep unwanted pets for two weeks and if they're not adopted, they put them to sleep."

"Put them to sleep," Louise said. She didn't know anybody said that anymore and here was her friend, Betsy, saying it.

"And these people never do. I've just heard about these places, I've never seen one. I don't think there are many of them but they are around."

"I don't like the sound of it, oddly enough," Louise said. She always wanted to talk about Broom with the others until they actually wanted to discuss him, then she didn't want to anymore.

"You know that same woman came into the florist's the other day to buy roses and I said to her, 'Oh no, has Buckie bitten someone again!' "

Louise's friends looked at her.

"And she said, 'I don't know what you're talking about.' " Louise laughed. "She was pretending she wasn't the same person."

It was close to summer now. One early evening after work, Louise was sitting in front of her house when a van driving slowly by pulled up across the street and a man got out.

Louise was startled to see him walk over to her. He was deeply tanned with a ragged haircut. The collar of his shirt was too big for him.

"How do you do, Louise," he said. "I'm Elliot's brother."

Louise cast herself back, remembering Elliot. She had more difficulty than usual picturing him but then she saw him. It was still him exactly. Powerful Elliot, almost gleaming, gleaming with life. Deceitful shine, she thought, deceitful flow . . . Finally she said to the man, "You don't look at all like Elliot."

He seemed to be waiting for her to say more. When she didn't, he said, "I've been ill and out of the country. I couldn't travel, travel was impossible, but I got here as soon as I was able. Elliot and I had quarreled, we hadn't spoken for two years, you couldn't imagine the pettiness of our quarrel, it was over nothing. My heart is broken, I will never forgive myself." He paused. He looked bewildered. "I heard that he had a dog and that you have the dog now and that it might be something of a burden to you. I'd like to have the dog. I'd like to buy it."

"I couldn't do that," Louise said simply.

"I insist on paying you something."

"But I won't give the dog up, it's impossible," Louise said. He could be a vivisectionist for all she knew. He might as well be a vivisectionist.

"It would mean a great deal to me," he said, his mouth trembling. "My brother's dog."

Louise shook her head.

"I can't believe this," he muttered. He spoke again patiently, as though she had utterly misunderstood his position and the seriousness of his request. His guilt was almost holy, he was on a holy quest. He had determined that this was what must be done, the only thing that remained possible now to do.

"We were so close," he said. "He was my little brother. I taught him how to ski, how to drive, we went to the same college. I'd always protected him, he looked up to me, then there was this stupid, senseless quarrel. Now he's gone forever and I'm all ruined inside; it's destroyed me, I'm broken." He rubbed his chest with his fingers as if there really was something broken there. "If I could care now for something he had cared for, I thought . . . this is what I thought—that I would have something of my brother, of my brother's love."

"I don't mean to sound rude," Louise said, "but we've all been dealing with this for some time now and you suddenly appear, having been ill and out of the country both at the same time. Both at the same time," she repeated, for it seemed unlikely. "It's just so unnecessary now, your appearance, don't you know . . . it's possible to come around too late."

"That's not true," he said. He was sallow beneath his tan. "Your friends, Elliot's friends, said they were sure you'd appreciate the opportunity, that they were sure you wouldn't mind, that you'd be relieved and delighted in fact."

"That just shows how little we comprehend one another," Louise said. "Even when we try," she added. "Have you ever had a dog before?" Louise was just curious. She didn't mean to lead him on, but as soon as she said this, she feared she had given him hope.

"Oh yes," he said eagerly, "as boys we always had dogs."

"They'd die and you'd get another?"

"That's not how I'd put it, that's a queer way of putting it," he said. "We knew how to take care of them, if that's what you mean, we took good care of them." His voice had risen.

"Look," Louise said, "your brother had this dog for about three minutes." She felt she was exonerating Elliot.

"It was more than three minutes. Three minutes," he said, bewildered.

"I said about three minutes. You should get a dog and pretend it was your brother's and care for it tenderly and that will be that. That's the solution." Louise was not going to get up and go inside the house and lock the door against him. She would wait him out. She wasn't afraid. She felt wise, even. "There's nothing more to discuss," she said.

He turned from her sadly. There were several youths peering into his van. "Get away from there!" he yelled. He hurried toward them.

"Owhhhhhh," one of them said, "don't bite us sir, please sir." They ambled away.

It was Walter's turn to give a party. He had a fire in the fireplace although it wasn't at all cold. Still, it was very pleasant, everyone said so.

"I ordered half a cord of wood but it wasn't split, it was just logs," Walter said, "and one of the logs had a chain partly imbedded in it, like a dog chain. The tree had started to grow right over the chain."

"Wow," Daisy said. She had a long blond chin hair that she liked to twist and was twisting at that moment. "I don't think so."

"Who would have thought that Elliot would have such a creepy brother," Angus said. "I wouldn't have given him the dog either."

"Still, I'm amazed you didn't, Louise," Jack said.

"I guess he got all the things we actually remembered Elliot having," Andrew said. "I remember a rather nice ship's clock, for instance. That wristwatch I was given, who'd ever seen that before? I don't think Elliot ever wore that watch."

"He wasn't in his right mind," Betsy said. "We keep forgetting that. He wasn't thinking clearly. If you're thinking clearly, you don't take your own life."

Again, Louise marveled at her friend's way of phrasing things. To take your own life was to take control of it, to take possession of it, give it a shape by occupying it. But Elliot's life still had no shape, even though it had been completed.

"I want to confess something," Andrew said. "I have tossed that watch." He had crammed it into an overflowing Goodwill bin in the parking lot of a shopping mall. He described the experience of pushing the watch into an open-throated softly bulging sack as an extremely unpleasant one. Everyone knew the Goodwill bin with its mute congregation of displaced things attending it, things too large to be slipped inside. All those things waiting to be revisited in this life, waiting to be found again. They seemed more hopeful than human beings.

Everyone drank too much that evening and began relating their most recent dreams. Wilbur had dreamed that he was in the middle of a highway, trying to cross, trying to cross with Daisy. Daisy said she used to have that dream but didn't anymore. Angus had dreamed he was in a coffee shop where a kindly but inefficient waitress who looked like his mother but so old, so impossibly old, kept directing him to a table that wasn't there. Jack had dreamed that he needed a liver transplant but wasn't on the list to get one. You have to be on the list, people kept saying in Jack's dream, just get on the list. Lucretia had dreamed that she was on a peculiarly shaped stage singing *Kindertotenlieder* as beautifully as Kathleen Ferrier but she had to assure her audience, which she could not see, that it was only a copy. Walter had dreamed that he was in church, kneeling at the communion rail in the silk pajamas.

"The cup was working its way toward me but then it became a thermometer and by the time it reached me it was a car's dipstick and the priest was a mechanic wiping it clean with a dirty cloth," Walter related.

"But that's just how you thought it was," Louise protested. "Your thoughts are trying to protect you from something, that's obvious."

No one asked what Louise's last dream had been. She had had the dog for six months now. When she realized how much time had passed, she thought, Six more months to go. She thought, In six months we'll know more.

Someone was putting a house up behind Louise's house. The yard had been bladed and most of the trees taken down. The pale, banal framework of a house stood there. When Louise gave a party, everyone was shocked at the change.

"I thought that yard went with this house," Jack said.

"Well, I guess not," Louise said.

"All those little birdhouses are gone," Lucretia said. "People put them inside now, you know, as a decorative accent. They paint them in these already fading, flaking colors and put them around."

"They're safer inside," Angus said.

"That thing is going to be huge, Louise," Betsy said. "It's going to loom over you."

They talked for awhile about what she could plant to block it out.

"Nothing will grow in time," Betsy said.

"In time for what?" Walter said.

"Everything takes so long to grow, my God, Louise," Betsy said, "you'd better just move."

"Louise," Daisy said, "if you die are you going to leave us anything?" She was sitting on the sofa with Wilbur. They were eating pretzels from their hands as though they were chewing soup. Outside, the wind was blowing hard but there were no trees anymore to indicate this with their tossing branches. A door blew open, banging, though.

Louise woke up the following morning, feeling purposeful. She was going to move. She wasn't going to watch that house going up behind her. Within a week, she had found another place. Walter and Lucretia helped her move. Walter had a little truck and they transferred all the furniture in one trip. They transferred Broom too with his dog bed and his dish for water and his dish for food. Then Louise packed her car with everything else. The car was packed right up to the roof. Even so, she had thrown away a lot of things, she was simplifying, purifying her life. She swept the old house clean, she was so glad to be leaving. She looked with satisfaction at the empty rooms, the stark windows and their newly ugly vistas. She slammed the door and headed for her car, but the car was not where she had left it. She stared at the place where it had been. But it had vanished, been stolen, everything was gone. The sun was bright, and still shining on the place where it had been.

It was Betsy's turn to have a party. They told theft stories, they all had them. They tried to cheer Louise up. She had already bought another car with the insurance money. It wasn't as appealing but she liked it in a different way. She liked it because she didn't like it that much, she wasn't as girlishly pleased with it as she had been with the other one. The other one had had that little bit of sparkle.

"You can get all new clothes," Lucretia said. "You can go on a spree. That favorite dress of yours had a spot on it anyway and kind of on the back at that."

"I got that spot out," Louise said. "It did not. I loved that dress."

"I bet you can't even remember everything you had packed in the car," Jack said.

"My pearls," Louise said sadly.

"Christmas is coming," Angus said. But he always said that, as though he were going to buy everyone wonderful gifts, the gifts of their most perfect desiring. But he only bought champagne and cookies and they would drink and eat was all.

"My grandmother's silver tea service."

"Louise, you know you never used that and would never use that in your life. It was a burden to you, it didn't have a place," Lucretia said.

"But it's gone," Louise said with great earnestness. She didn't know what she meant actually. It was gone, of course, but there was something else, something worse. She had made all these choices. She had discarded this and retained that and it hadn't mattered.

"Things are ephemeral," Daisy said.

"And an illusion," Wilbur said.

"Well which?" Jack demanded, annoyed. Everyone was a little embarrassed. Seldom did anyone respond to the twins. "I'll tell you one thing," Jack said, "I sold that crazy bowl of Elliot's to an antique store."

None of them could think about Elliot without being thwarted by the things he'd given them, the mystery of the things he'd given. His behavior had been inexplicable. It was all inexplicable.

"Oh, I can't think about it anymore!" Louise cried. They were all drinking margaritas out of silly glasses.

"How is Broom?" Andrew asked delicately.

"Oh, I've rather gotten used to Broom," Louise said.

Louise settled quickly into her new house. It was bigger than the other one and more ordinary. Broom didn't know which room to disappear into. He had tried them all. He couldn't decide. He would take up in the most unlikely places. Sometimes, she would come across him on the fifth step of a narrow back staircase. What an odd place to be! And he would look uncomfortably at her at these times, the way he always did. Still, she was sure Elliot would not have wanted her to surrender the animal so easily. Of course, she would never know Elliot's thoughts. She herself could only think— and she was sure she was like many others in this regard, it was her connection with others really—that life would have been far different under other circumstances, and yet here it wasn't, after all.

Two Poems by Daniel Kunitz

Geniza

> *In which members of a synagogue entomb virtually every piece of the community's writing to avoid desecrating God's name.*

Of all the notes, scraps and scribbles
Crushed in my fist for oblivion's food
(Not to spare the name of God—
I wasn't pious) yours I set
Apart, memorized. Syllables
Spurning in mordant tones of regret,
Squibs of passion . . . these are all
My marshaled senses can recall.

Now, though your missives may be lost,
Leaves slipped long ago between pages
In a book, like fading vestiges
Or questions pressed fine and brittle,
They'll still sway my life, last
In recollection's imperfect middle
Distance: a voice surging up
To conjugate our fractured hope.

Asleep in San Vito

Sicily

Had there been clouds, they would have shifted
As slowly as my thoughts. But no, the sky bubbled
Into lidless blue, leaving ample
Room for the effortless shuffle of sensation,
Sure successive waves licking me pebble-
Smooth and small. Eyes closed, untroubled
By flesh, I contracted to my soul's
Dense kernel.
             The high sun fired the cliffs
Until they stood like a cracked ochre cake
Shelving over us—a lone family
Baking with beached sea urchins
By the low-tide line. From yards off
Along the strand, a stranger would see us
Bend and ripple in the heat waves,
Stippled streaks of skin cooked
Raw, blushing rose.

I floated in the black sea that borders sleep.
Grown heavy with excess, with visions that prefigured
The vistas on this stone-strewn island,
Encumbered by all the extraneous events
Of a life spent collecting ostracons of elegance,
Shards from the broken vessel
Which once gathered my friends and me
In prolix communion,
I felt prepared for the paring,
To find, again in a dry and rugged landscape,
My own bleached spine.

Two Poems by Eric Ormsby

The Junkyard Vision of Jaham

In paradise the smell of engine oil
Will undercut the roses. The carburetors
Of Eden will distract the seraphim,
Those jukebox lutenists in phosphate trees.
The vaporous hush of essences
At the pinging pump will cauterize
The contusions of love, and the houris all
Will bask on velveteen and Naugahyde
Bucket seats in a Russian Leather breeze.

The camshafts of heaven will outlive the axle trees.
The music of the manifolds will gown the clouds.
I see the black-seamed fingertips of the mechanics
On the copper-colored keys of their accordions
And hear the ditties of the pit stops pool.
The music of paradise will be shirt-sleeved and cool
And brandish red bandannas of rough flannel.
The integrity of metals will marmorealize
Fleeting affections yet be various.
Amber oils will coronate chrome impulses
And be steadfast at last.

                The dark order
Of the mechanisms of heaven will be intricate
And unending, bedewed with rich grease
And yet, withal, imbued by the love
Of couplings and black
Gaskets, the grit of the known
Lingeringly delivered back to innocence.

A House in Winter

after Al-Sanawbari (died 945 in Baghdad)

Winter sweetens my house with its fragrance.
What could be better than a winter-sweetened house?

In platters heaped with food and in my good roof,
In plump cushions, in drapes brocaded with dark,
I find snug and continual pleasure against the cold.
And there is pleasure also in the courtyard pools
And their elegant pearling meander
Through gardens of grace, especially
On days when the sun-dimming clouds
Hammer against my walls,
And the drainpipes' voices, thick with slush,
Struggle to mimic the long-necked mandolins.
Then from within my house I watch other
Low-hanging clouds, pond-mesmerized,
Whittle slim-stemmed flagons from their subtle waves!

On evenings in my winter-sweetened house
The cup which the boy, fawn-delicate, displays
Apparels carnelian wine in winking crystal.
I adore the strands of hair at his temples and his brow
Where musk has darkened his head until his face
Shines out at me like the moon in a night of snow.

God has given the measures of winter and of summer.
You will not augment them, with all your scurrying.
Treasure your moment in this winter-gentled house!

Kevin Young

Homage to Phillis Wheatley

*Poet & Servant to Mr. Wheatley of Boston,
on her Maiden Voyage to Britain*

There are days I can understand
why you would want to board
broad back of some ship
and sail: venture, not homeward
but toward Civilization's

Cold seat,—having from wild
been stolen, and sent into more wild
of Columbia, our exiles
and Christians clamoring upon
the cobblestones of Bostontown—

Sail cross an Atlantic (this time) mild,
the ship's polite and consumptive
passengers proud. Your sickness
quit soon as you disembarked in mist
of England—free, finally, of our Republic's

Rough clime, its late converts who thought
they would not die, or die simply
in struggle, martyr to some God,—
you know of gods there
are many, who is really only

One—and that sleep, restless fever
would take most you loved. Why
fate fight? Death, dark mistress,
would come a-heralding silent
the streets,—no door to her closed,

No stair (servant or front) too steep.
Gen. Washington, whom you praise,
victorious, knows this—will even admit
you to his parlor. Who could resist a Negress
who can recite Latin and speak the Queen's?

Docked among the fog and slight sun
of London, you know who you are not
but that is little new. Native
of nowhere,—you'll stay a spell, return,
write, grow still. I wake with you

In my mind, leaning, learning
to write—your slight profile
that long pull of lower lip, its pout
proving you rescued by
some sadness too large to name.

My Most Excellence, my quill
and ink lady, you spill such script
no translation it needs—
your need is what's missing, unwritten
wish to cross back but not back

Into that land (for you) of the dead—
you want to see from above
deck the sea, to pluck from wind
a sense no Land can
give: drifting, looking not

For Leviathan's breath, nor waves
made of tea, nor for mermen half-
out of water (as you)—down
in the deep is not the narwhal enough real?
Beneath our wind-whipt banner you smile

At Sea which owns no country.

Two Poems by Rachel Loden

Bride of Tricky D.

Yorba Linda, California . . . Plans are afoot to exhume [Checkers], . . . died in 1964, and rebury him near the former president on the grounds of the Nixon presidential library.
—http://cnn.com/US/9704/27/briefs.pm/nixon.checkers/

And the rest is taps, or reveille. Maybe
he lies with dog & god

beneath the Yorba Linda pines, adrift
in history. There is no way

he's rumbling on about the next
campaign, how crack advance men

break & enter paradise while blasé
press fly back to Washington.

Somebody's shroud is in a twist
but it's so deadly smug out on the new

world order battlements. "Let's
slip the Constitution, Richard,

cut red ribbon on the virgin
century. Teach me tonight . . ." I find

his fierce beard lovely and the shadows
long. *Asleep with Pat & Checkers*

by his side . . . "We could do it,"
he'll say, "but it would be wrong."

My Exchange

> *irrational exuberance*
> —Alan Greenspan on the markets

Still, the path of the tango was not strewn
with roses. Five thousand years

might pass without a single dance, the dejecta
of great cities rolled out on a plain like dice

or jewels. And on my roof
the sleigh bells of the gods, their tchotchkes

curled inside a broken jar at Qumran, painted
standing armies in the vaults of heaven.

•

See also: TIMELINESS/UNTIMELINESS.
Was it some corporate *Sturmführer*

saw a need for spreadsheets
in a town like this, with seven central bankers

to look at; the sweet sea air buffeting
the NASDAQ? Oh irrational exuberance,

you make me weak! Let me lie among
the fallen orders, vermilion petals at my feet.

Alfred Corn

Who, What, Where, When, Why?

Rumor, the homemade metamorphosis;
That with each telling modifies its key
Adjectives, its semicolons; that scales
The afternoon, beyond the towers' *nth* floor,
A geyser of invention, a carnival
Lingo disseminated on winds of envy,
Calculation, itch for the fecund dirt.

No kangaroo court so summary as rumor,
Whose slurs and whispers frame a rougher justice,
Dispensing with the drab credential-check,
Skirting obstructive rules of evidence,
Always with an eye to the camera,
Always lobbying for conviction, however
Listless the testimony, however queasy.

Those times when prosecution aced its game?
A human metaphor stood for sentencing,
The lifelong upshot sealed in lead, since rumor
Makes no provisions for parole—or any
Amendment that might heal a broken statute.
Defendant reads a lot, no? Most of you do.
Some find the Stoic writings helpful. Try them.

Daniel Tobin

Floor Scrapers

after Caillebotte

What do you make of that odd one by the door,
his silk top hat and greatcoat folded
neatly beside his chair, a sketchbook flapped
over his knees, and his eyes: flint-gray, steady,
as if staring down his own death?

To him we are the shapes our bodies make
around themselves, the *scratch, scratch* of charcoal
ferreting its trail across the blank page.
When he is finished, will he have captured
the glisten of sweat down our shirtless backs,

the taut press of our arms at the work?
I think we will be like these ringlets, stripped
layers of pigment curling into themselves,
the window behind a frame of absence,
the floor, the whole room, awash in light.

But to be as stubbornly here as this stain!
Do you see? It's not him anymore but others
crowded there, and you and I before them
whispering together like confidants:
Soon, soon this canvas will be white again.

THE ISLAND was small, 1800 square miles, half a million people, but the population was very mixed and there were many separate worlds. When my father got a job on the local paper, we went to live in the city. It was only twelve miles away, but it was like going to another country.

Our little rural Indian world, the disintegrating world of a remembered India, was left behind. I never returned to it; lost touch with the language; never saw another Ramlila. In the city we were in a kind of limbo. Though the tropical houses were open to breeze and every kind of noise, and no one could be said to be private in his yard, we continued to live in our enclosed, self-sufficient way, we remained separate from the more colonial, more racially mixed life around us.

To go out to school, to arrive after two or three years at Mr Worm's exhibition class, cramming hard all the way, learning everything by heart, living with abstractions, having a grasp of very little, was like entering a cinema some time after the film had started and getting only scattered pointers to the story. It was like that for the twelve years I was to stay in the city before going to England. I saw people of other groups only from the outside; school friendships were left behind at school or in the street; it was the way people of our background had always lived. It never ceased to feel a stranger; I never fully understood where I was. I really never had the time to find out: all but nineteen months of those twelve years were spent in a blind, driven kind of colonial studying.

And I got to know very soon that there was a further world outside, of which our colonial world was only a shadow. This outer world — England principally, but also United States and Canada — ruled us in every way. It sent us governors and everything else we lived by: the special foods the island had needed since the slave days (smoked herrings, salted cod, condensed milk, New Brunswick sardines in oil); the special medicines (Dodd's Kidney Pills, Dr Sloan's Liniment, the tonic called Six Sixty-Six). It sent us the coins of England, from the halfpenny to the half-crown, to which we automatically gave values in our dollars and cents, one cent to a halfpenny. It sent us text books and examination question papers for the various school certificates (and even during the war students' scripts were sent back to England to be marked). It sent us films, and Life and Time. It sent folded packets of The Illustrated London News to Mr Worm's office. It sent us everything.

A manuscript page from "Reading and Writing," an unpublished essay.

V.S. Naipaul
The Art of Fiction CLIV

Sir Vidiadhar Surajprasad Naipaul was born on 17 August 1932 in Chaguanas, Trinidad, where his ancestors had emi-

grated from India—his maternal grandfather, at the turn of the century, had traveled from that country as an indentured servant.

Naipaul, in his essay "Prologue to an Autobiography" from Finding the Center, *has written: "Half a writer's work . . . is the discovery of his subject. And a problem for me was that my life had been varied, full of upheavals and moves: from grandmother's Hindu house in the country, still close to the rituals and social ways of village India; to Port of Spain, the negro and G.I. life of its streets, the other, ordered life of my colonial English school, which is called Queen's Royal College, and then Oxford, London and the freelances' room at the BBC. Trying to make a beginning as a writer, I didn't know where to focus."*

After two failed attempts at novels and three months before his twenty-third birthday, Naipaul found his start in the childhood memory of a neighbor in Port of Spain. The memory provided the first sentence for Miguel Street, *which he wrote over six weeks in 1955 in the BBC freelancers' room at the Langham Hotel, where he was working part-time editing and presenting a literary program for the Caribbean Service. The book would not be published until 1959, after the success of* The Mystic Masseur *(1957), which received the John Llewellyn Rhys Memorial Prize and* The Suffrage of Elvira *(1958), which was awarded the Somerset Maugham Award. A House of Mr. Biswas was published in 1961, and in 1971 Naipaul received the Booker Prize for* In a Free State. *Four novels have appeared since then:* Guerrillas *(1975),* A Bend in the River *(1979),* The Enigma of Arrival *(1987) and* A Way in the World. *Naipaul received a knighthood in 1990 for his service to literature.*

In the early 1960s, Naipaul began writing about his travels. He has written four books on India: The Middle Passage *(1962),* An Area of Darkness *(1964) and* India: A Wounded Civilization *(1977) and* India: A Million Mutinies Now *(1990).* The Return of Eva Peron *and* The Killings in Trinidad (*published in the same volume in 1980*) *recorded his experiences in Argentina, Trinidad and the Congo. Indonesia, Iran, Pakistan and Malaysia are the subject of* Among the Believers: An Islamic Journey *(1981). He returned to those countries in 1995;* Beyond Belief, *an account of those travels, was published this year.*

In conversation with Naipaul, one finds the issues and ideas are always highly subtle and complex—which he keeps reminding you, lest you see things only in monochrome—but the language steers clear of obfuscation and cant. Indeed Naipaul can be a difficult companion. The humbleness of his beginnings, the long struggles, the sheer scale of his artistic beginnings clearly have bred in him deep neuroses—at sixty-six, the neurotic circuitry is still buzzing. Despite the edginess, and the slight air of unpredictability it brings into any interaction with him, Naipaul proved to be an interviewer's delight.

The interview is culled from a series of conversations in New York City and India. Part of the interview was conducted (by Jonathan Rosen) at the Carlyle Hotel on 16 May 1994. Naipaul spent several minutes rearranging the furniture in the hotel suite in an effort to locate the chair best suited to his aching back. He has the habit of removing glasses before answering a question, though that only enhances his scrutinizing expression and attitude of mental vigilance. The occasion for the interview was the publication of A Way in the World, *but despite an initial wish to "stay with the book," Naipaul relaxed into a larger conversation that lasted several hours and touched on many aspects of his life and career.*

V.S. NAIPAUL

Let me know the range of what you are doing and how you are going to approach it. I want to know with what intensity to talk. Are we going to stay with the book?

INTERVIEWER

Would you like to?

NAIPAUL

It's a long career. There are many books. If things are to be interesting, it is better to be specific and focused. It's more stimulating to me, too.

INTERVIEWER

Was *A Way in the World* a difficult book to write?

NAIPAUL

In what way?

INTERVIEWER

There are so many different pieces to it, yet it fits together as a whole.

NAIPAUL

It was written as a whole—from page one to the end. Many writers tend to write summing-up books at the end of their lives.

INTERVIEWER

Were you conscious of trying to sum things up?

NAIPAUL

Yes. What people have done—people like Waugh, in his war trilogy, or Anthony Powell—is create a character like themselves to whom they can attach these reinterpreted adventures. Powell has a character running through his books who is like him but not him, because he doesn't play a dominant role. I think this is one of the falsities that the form imposes on people, and for many years I've been thinking how to overcome it.

INTERVIEWER

How to overcome . . .

NAIPAUL

You didn't understand what I was saying?

INTERVIEWER

I'm guessing that you mean the space between Marcel Proust the author and Marcel the narrator of *Remembrance of Things Past*.

NAIPAUL

No, I was thinking—well, yes, put it like that. I was thinking that to write about the war, which was a big experience for him, Waugh had to invent a Waugh character. Whenever I have had to write fiction, I've always had to invent a character who roughly has my background. I thought for many years how to deal with this problem. The answer was to face it boldly—not to create a bogus character but to create, as it were, stages in one's evolution.

INTERVIEWER

I'm struck by how much your autobiography overlaps with the vast history of the West. Do you have a sense that to write about yourself is to write about the larger world? Did you strive to achieve this relationship or did you find it naturally evolving?

NAIPAUL

Naturally, it had to evolve, because that's learning, isn't it? You can't deny what you've learned; you can't deny your travels; you can't deny the nature of your life. I grew up in a small place and left it when I was quite young and entered the bigger world. You have to contain this in your writing. Do you understand what I am saying?

INTERVIEWER

I do understand, but I was wondering about something a little different.

NAIPAUL

Try it again. Rephrase it. Make it simple and concrete so we can deal with it.

INTERVIEWER

I imagine you as having begun in a place that you were eager to leave but that has turned out—the more you studied it and returned to it—actually to be at the center of issues that are of enormous importance to the West. You call Trinidad a small place but, as you've written, Columbus wanted it, Raleigh wanted it . . . When did you become conscious of Trinidad as a focus of the desires of the West, and a great subject?

NAIPAUL

I have been writing for a long time. For most of that time people were not interested in my work, so my discoveries have tended to be private ones. If it has happened, it's just a coincidence. I wasn't aware of it. Also, it is important to note, the work has not been political or polemic. Such a work written in the 1950s would be dead now. One must always try to see the truth of a situation—it makes things universal.

INTERVIEWER

You mentioned that your readers are coming to you late: do you think that the world is now catching up with you? Is this a change in readership or a change in the world?

NAIPAUL

It's a change in the world. When I began to write, there were large parts of the world that were not considered worth writing about. Do you know my book *The Loss of El Dorado*? It contains all the research on Raleigh and Miranda. When it was published, the literary editor of a very important paper in London told me that I only should have written an essay because it wasn't a big enough subject. He was a foolish man. But it gives you an idea of how the world has changed.

INTERVIEWER

Do you think the world is more understanding now of the psychological displacement with which you deal?

NAIPAUL

It's such a widespread condition now. People still have the idea of the single cultural unit, which actually has never existed. All cultures have been mingled forever. Look at Rome: Etruria was there before, and there were city-states around Rome. Or the East Indies: people from India went out to found further India, then there was the Muslim influence . . . People come and go all the time; the world has always been in movement.

INTERVIEWER

Do you think you have become an exemplar of that mixed world?

NAIPAUL

I don't think so. I am always thinking about the book. You are writing to write a book: to satisfy that need, to make a living, to leave a fair record behind, to alter what you think is incomplete and make it good. I am not a spokesman for anybody. I don't think anybody would want me to be a spokesman.

INTERVIEWER

The three explorers in *A Way in the World* are drawn back to Trinidad at their peril. I sense from your earlier writing that you fear you might make one trip too many—that there is an annihilating aspect to that place from which you came, which might this time overwhelm you.

NAIPAUL

You mustn't talk like that. It's very frightening. I think I have made my trips there and I won't go back again.

INTERVIEWER

But imaginatively Trinidad does pull you.

NAIPAUL

No. I'm finished with it imaginatively. You see, a writer tries very hard to see his childhood material as it exists. The nature of that childhood experience is very hard to understand—it has a beginning, a distant background, very dark, and then it has an end when a writer becomes a man. The reason why this early material is so important is that he needs to understand it to make it complete. It is contained, complete. After that there is trouble. You have to depend on your intelligence, on your inner strength. Yes, the later work rises out of this inner strength.

INTERVIEWER

I am struck by your title *A Way in the World*. It reminds me of the end of *Paradise Lost*—wandering out after the expulsion. Is the world what you enter when you leave home?

NAIPAUL

I suppose it depends on the nature of where you live. I don't know whether it is a fair question or if it should be answered. Put it another way.

INTERVIEWER

I guess I'm asking what you mean by *world*.

NAIPAUL

People can live very simple lives, can't they? Tucked away, without thinking. I think the world is what you enter when you think—when you become educated, when you question—because you can be in the big world and be utterly provincial.

INTERVIEWER

Did you grow up with a larger idea of the world? An idea represented by the word *world*?

NAIPAUL

I always knew that there was a world outside. I couldn't accept that with which I grew up—an agricultural, colonial society. You cannot get any more depressing or limited.

INTERVIEWER

You left Trinidad in 1950 to study at Oxford—setting out across the seas to an alien land in pursuit of ambition. What were you looking for?

NAIPAUL

I wanted to be very famous. I also wanted to be a writer: to be famous for writing. The absurdity about the ambition was that, at the time, I had no idea what I was going to write about. The ambition came long before the material. The filmmaker Shyam Benegal once told me that he knew he wanted to make films from the age of six. I wasn't as precocious as he: I wanted to be a writer by the age of ten.

I went to Oxford on a colonial government scholarship, which guaranteed to see you through any profession you wanted. I could have become a doctor or an engineer, but I simply wanted to do English at Oxford—not because it was English and not because it was Oxford, but only because it was away from Trinidad. I thought that I would learn about myself in the three or four years I was going to be away. I thought that I would find out my material and miraculously become a writer. Instead of learning a profession, I chose this banality of English—a worthless degree, it has no value at all.

But I wanted to escape Trinidad. I was oppressed by the pettiness of colonial life and by (this relates more particularly to my Indian-Hindu family background) the intense family disputes in which people were judged and condemned on moral grounds. It was not a generous society—neither the colonial world nor the Hindu world. I had a vision that, in the larger world, people would be appreciated for what they were—people would be found interesting for what they were.

INTERVIEWER

Unconnected to the family from which they came?

NAIPAUL

Yes. I imagined that one would not be subject to that moralizing judgment all the time. People would find what you were saying interesting, or they would find you uninteresting. It actually did happen in England—I did find a more generous way of looking at people. I still find it more generous.

INTERVIEWER

Did you enjoy Oxford?

NAIPAUL

Actually, I hated Oxford. I hate those degrees and I hate all those ideas of universities. I was far too well prepared for it. I was far more intelligent than most of the people in my college or in my course. I am not boasting, you know well—time has proved all these things. In a way, I had prepared too much for the outer world; there was a kind of solitude and despair, really, at Oxford. I wouldn't wish anyone to go through it.

INTERVIEWER

Do you ever wonder what would have become of you if you had stayed in Trinidad?

NAIPAUL

I would have killed myself. A friend of mine did—out of stress, I think. He was a boy of mixed race. A lovely boy, and very bright. It was a great waste.

INTERVIEWER

Is he the boy that you mention in the introduction to *A House for Mr. Biswas*?

NAIPAUL

Yes, he is the boy I had in mind. We shared an admiration for each other. His death was terrible.

INTERVIEWER

Do you still feel the wounds of your early life?

NAIPAUL

I think about how lucky I was to escape. I think about how awful and oppressive it was. I see it now more clearly for what it was: the plantation—perhaps a part of the New World but entirely autonomous. No doubt I've healed the wounds because I have thought about it so much. I think about how lucky I was not to have been destroyed utterly. There has been a life of work since then, a life of endeavor.

INTERVIEWER

Why has writing always been the central need of your life—the way out of everything?

NAIPAUL

It was given to me as an ambition. Or rather, I took my father's example; he was a writer—a journalist, but he also wrote stories. This was very important to me. My father examined our Hindu background in his stories. He found it a very cruel background, and I understood from his stories that it was a very cruel world. So I grew up with the idea that it is important to look inwards and not always define an external enemy. We must examine ourselves—our own weaknesses. I still believe that.

INTERVIEWER

You have said that you see writing as the only truly noble calling.

NAIPAUL

Yes, for me it is the only noble calling. It is noble because it deals with the truth. You have to look for ways of dealing with your experience. You have to understand it and you have to understand the world. Writing is a constant striving after a deeper understanding. That is pretty noble.

INTERVIEWER

When did you start writing?

NAIPAUL

I started work on a novel in 1949. It was a very farcical, a very interesting idea: a black man in Trinidad giving himself a name of an African king. This is the idea I tried to explore. It dragged on as a piece of writing for two years because I was too young to know much. I began it a little bit before I left home and finished it during a long vacation from Oxford. I was very glad I did finish it because at least it gave me the experience of finishing a long book. Of course nothing happened to it.

Then, after I left Oxford, really in great conditions of hardship, I began to write something intensely serious. I was trying to find my own voice, my tone—what was really me and not borrowed or acting. This serious voice led me into great shallows of depression, which dragged on for a while until I was told to abandon it by someone to whom I had sent the manuscript. He told me it was rubbish; I wanted to kill him but deep down in my heart I knew he was absolutely right. I spent many weeks feeling wretched because it had been five years and nothing was happening. There was this great need to write, you see. I had decided it was to be my livelihood—I had committed my life to it. Then something happened: out of that gloom, I hit upon my own voice. I found the material that was my own voice; it was inspired by two literary sources: the stories of my father and a Spanish picaresque novel, the very first published, in 1554, *Lazarillo Tormes*. It is a short book about a little poor boy growing up in imperial Spain, and I loved its tone of voice. I married these two things together and found that it fitted my personality: what became genuine and original and mine really was fed by these two, quite distinct sources.

INTERVIEWER

This is when you began writing *Miguel Street*?

NAIPAUL

Yes. It is immensely hard to be the first to write about anything. It is always easy afterwards to copy. So the book I wrote—that mixture of observation and folklore and newspaper cuttings and personal memory—many people can do, but at the time it was something that had to be worked out.

Imagine writing a book like *Miguel Street* in 1955. Today

people are interested in writing from India or other former colonies, but at the time it was not considered writing. It was very hard to have this book with me for four years before it was published. It really upset me and it is still a great shadow over me.

INTERVIEWER

You had written two books by 1955, *The Mystic Masseur* and *Miguel Street*, but the first book was not published until 1957 and the stories not until 1959.

NAIPAUL

My life was very hard. When you are young, when you are destitute, when you wish to make known your presence in the world, two years is a very long time to wait. I was really made to suffer. Then *The Mystic Masseur* was finally published and it was dismissed by my own paper—I was working at the *New Statesman* at the time, where an Oxford don—quite famous later, described it as a little savory from a colonial island. A little savory, which didn't represent labor.

It would be interesting to see the books that were considered real books by the reviewers at that time. It is useless to tell me now, "All right, the books have been around for forty years, they are still printed." I was damaged. I was wounded by this neglect. People today have it much easier, which is why they complain. I never complained, I just had to go on.

INTERVIEWER

You must have been sustained largely by self-belief?

NAIPAUL

Yes. I never doubted. From the time I was a child, I had the feeling that I was marked.

INTERVIEWER

You started writing *A House for Mr. Biswas* just as your first novel was published.

NAIPAUL

Yes. I was casting around in a desperate way for a subject. It was so despairing that I actually began to write with a pencil—I didn't feel secure enough. The idea I had involved someone like my father, who at the end of his life would be looking at the objects by which he is surrounded and considering how they came into his life. I wrote laboriously without inspiration for a very long time—about nine months.

INTERVIEWER

Did you write every day?

NAIPAUL

Not strictly every day because when you are not inspired you do things with a heavy heart. Also, I was trying at the same time to become a reviewer. Someone had recommended me to the *New Statesman*—they sent me one thing and then another, but I was trying too hard and it failed. Then they sent me some books on Jamaica, and this nice, easy voice came to me. So there was some achievement at the time—learning how to write short, interesting pieces about a book and to make the book absolutely real to the reader. Eventually, the novel caught fire and thereafter it was all right. I began to devote three weeks out of every four to this work. I think that I knew pretty soon that it was a great work. I was very pleased that, although I was so young, I was committing myself to a major piece of writing because I had begun rather small—thinking that only when one had trained oneself enough would one attempt grand work. If someone had stopped me on the street and said, "I'll give you a million pounds now on one condition: you must not finish your book," I would have told him to go away. I knew I must finish my book.

INTERVIEWER

How was the book received?

NAIPAUL

It was received well from the moment it was read by the publisher. It would be nice to say that there was a rush on the book when it was published, but of course there wasn't. It would be nice to say that the world stood up and took notice, but of course the world didn't. The book just clanked along in the way of my earlier books, and it was some time before it made its way.

INTERVIEWER

A House for Mr. Biswas was a departure from your first three books, which were social comedies—you moved away from light, frothy comedy toward a more grim and serious tone.

NAIPAUL

Actually the tone is not grim. The book is full of comedy. Perhaps the comedy is less verbal, less farcical but it is in everything, I assure you. I can read a page of my writing from any book, however dark you might think it is, and you will laugh. The jokes have become deeper; the comedy has become more profound. Without the humorous view, you couldn't go on. You can't give a dark, tragic view all the time—it must be supported by this underlying comedy.

INTERVIEWER

I'd like to read you a sentence from *A Way in the World*: "It was that idea of the absurd never far away from us that preserved us. It was the other side of that anger and the passion that made the crowd burn the black policeman . . ." It reminds me of the humor in your early books about Trinidad and the other side of that humor—hysteria—in the books that followed.

NAIPAUL

It's very curious, isn't it—the same people who burned a policeman alive would dance and sing and tell a funny story about it.

INTERVIEWER

I was particularly struck by the word *us*—your inclusion of yourself in that situation.

NAIPAUL

Well, it was in Port of Spain. It has to be *us* because one is growing up in that atmosphere. It was our idea of the absurd, which comes out in the calypso—it's African, this idea of the absurd. It is something in late life I have come to understand—the hysteria and the sense of the absurd.

INTERVIEWER

And appreciate it more?

NAIPAUL

I'm more frightened by it. Understanding that the people who can be so absurd and write such funny songs also have a capacity for burning policemen. I fear cruelty.

INTERVIEWER

I can't help noticing that *A Way in the World* ends, like *The Enigma of Arrival*, with a funeral.

NAIPAUL

That was pure accident. I probably didn't think of it until you told me now. What I was aware of, as I was writing, was an emphasis on dead bodies and funerals and corpses. It begins with a man dressing a corpse and goes on to corpses in the Red House, where I worked, and there are lots of corpses in the Raleigh story.

INTERVIEWER

Is that a growing sense of mortality or is that a sense of the way of the world?

NAIPAUL

Probably it's facing it more boldly when one is older. When one is young, one has ways of dealing. Really, this is the physical thing of dying—I don't know what prompts it. It is for the reader to assess it; the writer mustn't judge himself.

INTERVIEWER

Are you conscious of reworking the elements of earlier fiction?

NAIPAUL

Yes. Getting the angle right: having acquired the material, writing about it another way and so producing new material.

INTERVIEWER

Would you agree that your later fiction takes a gentler angle? It seems to me that you now have a more accepting approach.

NAIPAUL

Be concrete. Where am I rough? Where have you found me harsh? Give me an example.

INTERVIEWER

Well, *In a Free State*.

NAIPAUL

That book was written out of great pain and very personal stress. It was written very carefully—put together like a watch or a piece of engineering. It is very well made. In 1979, for the first time, I was asked to give a reading in New York and, at the moment of the reading, I was aware of the extraordinary violence of the work—I didn't know it until then, so it wasn't conscious. I was shocked by the violence. When the jokes were made, people laughed; but what followed immediately stopped them. It was a very unsettling experience. Probably that reflects the way it was created—out of personal pain related to my own life, my own anguish.

INTERVIEWER

Can you describe the way you write?

NAIPAUL

I write slowly.

INTERVIEWER

Always?

NAIPAUL

I used to write faster when I was younger—about one thousand words a day when I was really going. I can't do that now. Now, on a good day, I write about three hundred words—very little.

INTERVIEWER

Do you ever not write?

NAIPAUL

Very often. Most days are like that.

INTERVIEWER

Hemingway called a day he had not written a day closer to death.

NAIPAUL

I'm not romantic like that. I just feel rather irritated. But I'm wise enough now and experienced enough to know that it will be all right. If it's in my head, it'll come out all right eventually. It's just finding the right way.

INTERVIEWER

Do you think language should only convey and not, as with John Updike, dance and dazzle?

NAIPAUL

Well, people have to do what they want to do. I wish my prose to be transparent: I don't want the reader to stumble over me; I want him to look through what I'm saying to what I'm describing. I don't want him ever to say, "Oh, goodness, how nicely written this is." That would be a failure.

INTERVIEWER

So even as the ideas are complex, the prose stays uncluttered.

NAIPAUL

Simple, yes. Also, I mustn't use jargon. You are surrounded by jargon—in the newspapers, in friends' conversations—and as a writer, you can become very lazy. You can start using words lazily. I don't want that to happen. Words are valuable. I like to use them in a valuable way.

INTERVIEWER
Do you despair for English literature?

NAIPAUL
No, I don't despair for it. It doesn't exist now, partly because it is very hard to do again what has been done before. It is in a bad, bad way in England. It has ceased to exist—but so much has existed in the past, perhaps there is no cause for grief.

INTERVIEWER
What about writers emerging from India? Do you feel the same about them?

NAIPAUL
I haven't examined that, but I think India will have a lot of writing. For many centuries India has had no intellectual life at all. It was a ritualized society, which didn't require writing. But when such societies emerge from a purely ritualistic life and begin to expand industrially, economically and in education, then people begin to need to understand what is happening. People turn to writers, who are there to guide them, to provoke them, to stimulate them. I think there will be a lot of writing in India now. The situation will draw it out.

INTERVIEWER
To return to the question of violence, I'd like to read a passage from *A Way in the World*: "I had grown up thinking of cruelty as something always in the background. There was an ancient, or not-so-ancient, cruelty in the language of the streets: casual threats, man to man and parents to children, of punishments and degradation that took you back to plantation times."

NAIPAUL
Yes. You always heard people saying things in calm language that were what the driver would have said to the slave:

I'll beat you till you pee, I'll take the skin off your back. These were awful things to hear, don't you think?

INTERVIEWER

Yet you have always resisted simplifying the anger—blaming it on colonialism or on the white masters of black slaves. There is no easy villain for you.

NAIPAUL

Of course there is no easy villain. These are safe things to say. They're not helpful in any way, they're not additions to any argument or discussion. They are just chants. Blaming colonialism is a very safe chant. These people would have been very quiet in colonial days; they would have been prepared for a life of subordination. Now that there is no colonialism, they speak very fearlessly. But other people were fearless long before.

INTERVIEWER

You have been criticized for running into the arms of the oppressor.

NAIPAUL

Who's criticized me?

INTERVIEWER

Derek Walcott, for one.

NAIPAUL

I don't know. I don't read these things. You mustn't ask me, you must ask him. You must judge these things yourself. I can't deal with all these things. It's been a long career.

INTERVIEWER

I'd like to ask . . .

NAIPAUL

You shouldn't have asked me that question about running to the British and the masters . . . Does it show in my work?

INTERVIEWER

I wouldn't say so.

NAIPAUL

Then why did you ask it?

INTERVIEWER

Because you always have resisted the simplifications but you have been surrounded by critics who have not resisted them.

NAIPAUL

Well, that's their problem. Have you read my book *The Middle Passage*? That book tells black people they can't be white people, which caused immense offense. In 1962, black people thought that because independence was coming, they had become closer to white people.

INTERVIEWER

The Middle Passage was your first attempt at nonfiction.

NAIPAUL

It is wrong to think of anyone as a producer of fiction because there is a limited amount of material you can work on. Yet to be a writer is to be observing, to be feeling and to be sensitive all the time. To be a serious writer is not to do what you have done before, to move on. I felt the need to move on. I felt I couldn't do again what I had done before—I shouldn't just stay at home and pretend to be writing novels. I should move and travel and explore my world—and let the form take its own natural course. Then a happy thing: a racial government, thinking they should give an appearance of being nonracial, invited me to come back and travel around the region. That's how I began to travel, and how I wrote *The Middle Passage*.

INTERVIEWER

You travel to India often. You first visited thirty-five years ago and keep coming back, both to write and to holiday. What is the source of your continuing fascination with India?

NAIPAUL

It is my ancestry, really, because I was born with a knowledge of the past that ended with my grandparents. I couldn't go beyond them, the rest was just absolute blankness. It's really to explore what I call the area of darkness.

INTERVIEWER

Do you think it is crucial to your function and material as a writer to know where you came from and what made you what you are?

NAIPAUL

When you're like me—born in a place where you don't know the history, and no one tells you the history, and the history, in fact, doesn't exist or, in fact, exists only in documents—when you are born like that, you have to learn about where you came from. It takes a lot of time. You can't simply write about the world as though it is all there, all granted to you. If you are a French or an English writer, you are born to a great knowledge of your origins and your culture. When you are born like me, in an agricultural colony far away, you have to learn everything. The writing has been a process of inquiry and learning for me.

INTERVIEWER

You have written three books on India over the last thirty-five years: *An Area of Darkness*, *A Wounded Civilization* and *A Million Mutinies Now*. Your response to the country has varied with each book.

NAIPAUL

Actually, the three books stand. Please understand that I do not want any one to supersede another. All three books stand because I think that they all remain true. The books are written in different modes: one is autobiographical, one is analytical and the last is an account of the people's experience in that country. They were written at different times and, of course, like India, people exist in different times. So you could say that *An Area of Darkness* is still there—the analysis of the invasions and defeat, the psychological wound, is still there. With the *Mutinies* book, in which people are discovering some little voice with which to express their personality and speak of their needs—that remains true. The books have to be taken as a whole—as still existing, still relevant, still important.

In all of this, you must remember that I am a writer—a man writing a paragraph, a chapter, a section, a book. It is a craft. I am not just a man making statements. So the books represent the different stages of my craft. *An Area of Darkness* is an extraordinary piece of craft—an extraordinary mix of travel and memory and reading. *A Million Mutinies Now* represents the discovery that the people in the country are important. It's a very taxing form, in the way that a lot happens during the actual traveling—a lot happens when you meet people. If you don't know how to talk to them, if you don't know how to get them to talk to you, there is no book. You use your judgment and your flair. I look at this and then that person, what he says about himself . . . His experiences lead you to consider something else and then something else and so on. The book happens during the actual traveling, although the writing takes time, as always. So the books are different bits of craft—always remember that I am a craftsman, changing the craft; I am trying to do new things all the time.

INTERVIEWER

Do you use a tape recorder when you interview people for your nonfiction?

NAIPAUL

I never use a recorder. It shortens the labor and makes the whole thing more precise—it puts me in control. Also, people find it hard to believe, but an hour and a half with anyone is as much as any text of mine can take.

INTERVIEWER

Do you begin an interview as soon as you meet a person?

NAIPAUL

First I'd meet you and talk to you; then I'd ask to come and see you. In ninety minutes, I can get two or three thousand words. You'll see me writing by hand and you'll speak slowly and instinctively. Yet it will be spoken and have the element of speech.

INTERVIEWER

An Area of Darkness suggests a lot of anger, as does much of your journalism about India. Do you think anger works better than understanding for a writer?

NAIPAUL

I don't like to think of it as journalism—journalism is news, an event that is important today. My kind of writing tries to find a spring, the motives of societies and cultures, especially in India. This is not journalism. Let me correct that—it is not something that anybody can do. It's a more profound gift. I'm not competing with journalists.

INTERVIEWER

But does anger work better than understanding?

NAIPAUL

I think it isn't strictly anger alone. It is deep emotion. Without that deep emotion there is almost no writing—then you do journalism. When you are deeply churned up, you know that you cannot express this naked raw emotion; you have to come to some resolution about it. It is this refinement of emotion, what you call understanding, that really makes the writing. These two things are not opposed to one another—understanding derives from what you call anger. I would call it emotion, deep emotion. Emotion is necessary to writing.

INTERVIEWER

I want to ask a question that comes from reading *An Area of Darkness*. You write about the Hindu idea that the world is illusion, which seems enormously attractive and, at the same time, terrifying to you. I'm wondering if I read that right?

NAIPAUL
I think you put your finger on it. It is both frightening and alluring. People can use it as an excuse for inactivity—when things are really bad and you are in a mess, it can be comforting to possess and enter that little chamber of thought where the world is an illusion. I find it very easy to enter that mode of thinking. It was with me for some weeks before writing *A Bend in the River*. I had the distinct sense of the world as an illusion—I saw it spinning in space as though I really had imagined it all.

INTERVIEWER
You have been to so many places—India, Iran, West Africa, the American Deep South. Are you still drawn to travel?

NAIPAUL
It gets harder, you know. The trouble is that I can't go places without writing about them. I feel I've missed the experience. I once went to Brazil for ten days and didn't write anything. Well, I wrote something about Argentina and the Falklands, but I didn't possess the experience—I didn't work at it. It just flowed through me. It was a waste of my life. I'm not a holiday taker.

INTERVIEWER
Didn't Valéry say that the world exists to be put in a book? Do you agree?

NAIPAUL
Or to be thought about, to be contemplated. Then you enjoy it, then it means something. Otherwise you live like a puppy: woof woof, I need my food now, woof woof.

INTERVIEWER
Your new book, *Beyond Belief*, returns to the subject of Islam, which you also examined in *Among the Believers*. Do

you anticipate any trouble from the prickliness of Islam's defenders with the book's publication?

INTERVIEWER

NAIPAUL

People might criticize me, but I am very careful never to criticize a faith or articles of a faith. I am just talking now about the historical and social effects. Of course, all one's books are criticized, which is how it should be. But remember this is not a book of opinion. This goes back to my earlier point about all one's work standing together: in the books of exploration that I have been writing, I've been working toward a form where, instead of the traveler being more important than the people he travels among, the people are important. I write about the people I meet—I write about their experiences and I define the civilization by their experiences. This is a book of personal experiences, so it will be very difficult to fault in the way you said because you can't say that it is maligning anything. I looked at personal experiences and made a pattern. In one way, you might simply say that it is a book of stories. It is a book of tales.

INTERVIEWER

Much in the way of *A Turn in the South* and *A Million Mutinies Now*?

NAIPAUL

Absolutely, yes. This book was a different challenge because I am very particular about not repeating a form, and here there were thirty narratives, which I tried to do differently—each one differently so that the reader would not understand the violation that was being done him. I didn't want the stories to read alike.

INTERVIEWER

Are you drained when you finish a book?

NAIPAUL

Yes, one is drained. These careers are so slow—I write a book and at the end of it I am so tired. Something is wrong

"The Paris Review remains the single most important little magazine this country has produced."

—T. Coraghessan Boyle

THE PARIS REVIEW

Enclosed is my check for:

☐ $34 for 1 year (4 issues)
(All payment must be in U.S. funds. Postal surcharge of $10 per 4 issues outside USA)

☐ $60 for 2 years

Bill this to my Visa/MasterCard:
Sender's full name and address needed for processing credit cards.

_____
Card number   Exp. date

☐ New subscription   ☐ Renewal subscription
☐ New address

Name _____
Address _____
City _____ State _____ Zip code _____

Please send gift subscription to:
Name _____
Address _____
City _____ State _____ Zip code _____
Gift announcement signature _____
call (718)539-7085

Please send me the following:

☐ The Paris Review T-Shirt   ($15.00)
   Color _____ Size _____ Quantity _____
☐ The following back issues: Nos. _____
   See listing at back of book for availability.

Name _____
Address _____
City _____ State _____ Zip code _____

☐ Enclosed is my check for $ _____
☐ Bill this to my Visa/MasterCard:

_____
Card number   Exp. date

Give The Paris Review!

BUSINESS REPLY MAIL

FIRST-CLASS MAIL PERMIT NO. 3119 FLUSHING, NY

POSTAGE WILL BE PAID BY ADDRESSEE

**THE PARIS REVIEW
45-39 171 PL
FLUSHING NY 11358-9892**

NO POSTAGE
NECESSARY
IF MAILED
IN THE
UNITED STATES

BUSINESS REPLY MAIL

FIRST-CLASS MAIL PERMIT NO. 3119 FLUSHING, NY

POSTAGE WILL BE PAID BY ADDRESSEE

**THE PARIS REVIEW
45-39 171 PL
FLUSHING NY 11358-9892**

NO POSTAGE
NECESSARY
IF MAILED
IN THE
UNITED STATES

with my eyes; I feel I'm going blind. My fingers are so sore that I wrap them in tape. There are all these physical manifestations of a great labor. Then there is a process of just being nothing—utterly vacant. For the past nine months, really, I've been vacant.

INTERVIEWER

Does something begin to agitate you to get back to writing?

NAIPAUL

I actually find myself being agitated now. I want to get back to my work.

INTERVIEWER

Do you have a new project in mind?

NAIPAUL

I'm unusual in that I have had a long career. Most people from limited backgrounds write one book. I'm a prose writer. A prose book contains many thousands of sentiments, observations, thoughts—it is a lot of work. The pattern for most people is to do a little thing about their own lives. My career has been other. I found more and more to write. If I had the strength, I probably would do more; there is always more to write about. I just don't have the energy, the physical capacity. You know, one can spend so many days now being physically wretched. I'm aging badly. I've given so much to this career for so long. I spend so much time trying to feel well. One becomes worn out by living, by writing, by thinking.

Have you got enough now?

INTERVIEWER

Yes.

NAIPAUL

Do you think I've wasted a bit of myself talking to you?

INTERVIEWER

Not, of course, how I'd put it.

NAIPAUL
You'll cherish it?

INTERVIEWER
You don't like interviews.

NAIPAUL
I don't like them because I think that thoughts are so precious you can talk them away. You can lose them.

—Tarun Tejpal
Jonathan Rosen

Our Lady of Beauty

Louis de Bernières

The sepulchre was situated in the communal graveyard of Santa Madre de Jesús in the province of Santander. This graveyard was, on account of its location upon the side of the volcano, almost unique in that everybody was buried upright and above ground, enclosed by four slabs glued poorly together by a pinkish mortar ground from tufa and mixed with lime and water. Often this mortar would crack and crumble away, so that by the light of a match or a taper the local children could peer into the darkness of the tombs and wonder at what they saw. Inside, they would behold the mummified ancestors of the village, draped with spiderwebs and often with snakes coiled around them, they would discern wisps of gossamer-like hair sprouting thinly from yellow scalps so shrunken that through the rents one could see white bone. There were shriveled lips drawn back in the parody of smiles and snarls, and one could wobble the teeth in their sockets by poking at them with a stick.

Sometimes one could see a cloth around the jaw, knotted at the top of the head to prevent the mouth from falling open, and some of the corpses had coins in the eyes for the payment of the boatman who ferries souls across the last waters. Occasionally, for a reason unknown, the corpse's head would have turned so that when one peeped through the chinks one's heart would leap to the throat with the horror of discovering that the cadaver was staring back as though it had been waiting there for years for a glimpse of the light in living eyes. There was one child in the pueblo who, having seen this, was pursued relentlessly by nightmares until one night she ran shrieking from her father's house and was lost in the maw of an opportunistic jaguar. Her grave is out on the edge of the cemetery, and is so small that one can lift off the lid at the top and see the pathetic pile of scored bones held together with the leather thongs of ligament and cartilage. Sometimes her father lifts it off himself to place orchids and blossoms of bougainvillea within, and he raises the skull in his hands and talks to it, kissing the lips and tenderly arranging what is left of the long dark hair. In this way he overcomes the tragedy of separation and accustoms himself to death.

We are a village accustomed to death. Every generation has borne witness to a new devastation. In my grandfather's time there was the plague of cholera that swept away all of his relatives, and the village was so cruelly emptied that he had to marry somebody from another place. In my father's time there was the violence, when there was one band of political guerrillas after another coming through, raping, robbing and murdering, starting and continuing vendettas that flare up all over again to this very day. In my village no one votes in elections anymore because of the memory of what outrages ensue from political idealism; when the communists tried to start a *foco* here we gave them away to the army, and then we got rid of the army by telling them that there were more communists towards San Isidro. We don't want any politics anymore, and, if we voted, it would be a vote to be left alone.

OUR LADY OF BEAUTY

In my own time we had the whooping cough that carried away one half of the children here and left so many empty cradles and broken hearts, and there was the avalanche when the south escarpment of the volcano broke away and flattened the end of the village where the brothel was. They say it was a judgment of God upon a house of infamy, but it carried away a good many fine men and women in addition to the revelers, not all of whom were very bad in any case. I might add that many of the whores survived, and that one of the dead was the priest, who had gone there to preach against the immoralities. It is because of the illogicality of God that around here we still worship the *orishas*, whom we can at least understand.

Above all, it is our cemetery that accustoms us to death. We grow up with our dead still visible among us, and one of them in particular. His name is Don Salvador, and he came here as a missionary about 150 years ago. He lived here for 40 years among us and had many fine children by various women; they say he was still a fine seducer even in his seventies, and when he died we made him a saint. It was not only out of gratitude for saving us from the damnation of the hell of the heathens, but also because he taught us so many things. He instructed us in writing and reading, he taught us Spanish, he taught us how to build bridges supported upon columns and he taught us the art of making love. Before he came it was forbidden to make love in any position except with the man on top, but he instructed the local women in the use of the tongue and in the differing possibilities for positions. He taught that if God had proscribed these positions He would have constructed our bodies in such a way that they would have been impossible to perform, and very soon the old ways were abandoned. It is because of him that I am called Dominico.

But the principle reason why we made him a saint was that he was so fertile. We remember not only his many children and his bull's appetite for love, but we have been told by our grandparents that wherever he passed the flowers burst into bloom, the crops burgeoned, the trees grew heavy with fruit, and women and animals grew heavy with the unborn.

So when he died they never sealed up his tomb, but only placed the slab in front of it, in a groove that was chiseled out of the rock. The path to his resting place is worn smooth by those who have crawled to it on hands and knees to beg for children. One would slide the stone away and kiss his feet and his hands, begging his intercession with Our Lady of Conception. A garland of flowers would be always upon his head and, despite the temptation to steal parts of him as holy relics, I have to say that nobody ever did, and he is still intact to this day. As a man there are things to which ordinarily I would not admit, but such is my devotion to Don Salvador that I state that it was he who cured me of my impotence with my wife, and I know many others for whom he has done the same, whose names I will not tell you in case it brings them shame.

In addition to Don Salvador's continued presence among us in his tomb, we carry him upon a litter around our fields twice a year when we do our planting. We sing hymns and songs, and we throw jugs of water on the ground, and it must be said that despite all the disasters we have suffered in the past, our crops, our animals and our women have never failed us, except for the time when the new priest forbade us to perform the ceremony, saying that it was a pagan sacrilege. Nowadays nobody pays any attention to the new priest, and not just because of this.

Don José always contradicted the teaching of Don Salvador. He has even told us that Don Salvador must have been an imposter and an Antichrist. Don José wants us to be ashamed of our bodies and to go back to the practice of making love furtively in only one position, he wants us to stop using herbs to avoid unwanted pregnancies, and he wants to frighten us with stories about infernos of fire when we are dead. But we remember the teachings of Don Salvador that have been passed down to us, and we argue with Don José, saying that we have been told about God being a God of Love. When we pass Don José in the street we say, "Be joyful in the Lord," and his face just grows more sorrowful. We do not like to see a man so lonely, but that is the price of his perversity.

It happened one evening that there was an earthquake. It was not a serious one, even though it seemed terrifying at the time. There was a distant rumble like thunder, and everything started to shake and sway. In my hut the tin mug slid off the shelf and fell onto my wife, and the bell in the porch of the church began to ring on its own. Some of the animals panicked, and there was a bull who escaped from his corral and ended up entangled in the creepers at the edge of the forest. Everybody ran into the street, and most of us could not keep our balance, so we all fell over. Old Aldonaldo remained in his hammock smoking a *puro* and laughing at us, and he seemed to be the only stationary object in a world that had become as restless as the sea. He was calling out, "Ay, ay, ay," and enjoying every minute of it.

As it was the dry season, a great cloud of dust got shaken up, and we all got covered from head to toe in white dust. We were all coughing and falling about when Don José ran out of his house crying out, "Repent, repent, the Kingdom of God is at hand. Woe to the inhabiters of the earth and of the sea, for the devil is come down unto you, having great wrath, because he knoweth that he hath but a short time." No one was more disappointed than Don José to discover afterwards that there had been no damage to speak of.

In fact the only damage was to the cemetery, where the slabs in the front of the tombs had in most cases fallen away. In some of them the bodies had fallen out forwards and were splayed upon the ground like withered drunkards or like the casualties of a battle, but in most of them the dead were still upright.

We wandered about the cemetery awestruck. The corpses seemed to be leaning casually against the sides of their habitations, and despite their mummification, their yellowness, the transparency of their skin, and the whiteness of their bones, they seemed extraordinarily full of life, all except the recent corpses, which reeked horribly and dripped with a foul slime whose color and odor comes back to me in bad dreams. We put the slabs back on those ones first, partly because of the offense to relatives, partly because of the stink and partly because the vultures were showing an interest. Afterwards they perched forlornly on top of the graves, reminding me of how I felt when I could not crack a Brazil nut as a child.

Seeing the corpses brought the village back to its history. There were people there who had been all but forgotten, but now the living were wandering among them, recognizing shreds of clothing, characteristic missing teeth, seeing the machete cuts of old murders, the broken bones of accidents. We were saying, "Ay, that is Alfonso who lived by the river, who got bitten by the mad dog and who was in love with Rosalita," and, "Ay, ay, there is Mahoma, who arrived from nowhere with his strange religion and took four wives, and there is the holy book written in squiggles that he carried about with him and that he read from the back to the front," and, "Look, this is Saba who was so beautiful that two men killed themselves out of love for her, and then she took up with Rafael who had only one arm." It made many old folk happy to see their old friends again.

But one man was more strangely affected. In the oldest part of the cemetery a grave had opened, the identity of whose occupant nobody could fathom, and who was a miracle.

She had her eyes closed and she was very beautiful. People nowadays when they tell this story always say that she was in a perfect state and that she was as fresh as the day before she died. They will tell you that her lips were as moist as if she had just eaten a mango, and that she smelled of flowers and of vanilla, but that is not exactly how I remember it. I recall that her lips were dry, as they are when one wakes on a hot morning, and that she smelled of a house that has been shut up and never cleaned for years. People will tell you that her limbs were supple and full, whereas I recall them having the stiffness of an old lady's. Otherwise, what they will tell you is mostly true.

OUR LADY OF BEAUTY

I suppose it is possible that two centuries of death might have turned a dark woman white, but it seemed to us that she was a white lady because her skin was white like the flesh of a cassava, she had restrained lips, and her hair, although it was black, was very long and straight. Also she was tall, and so she could not have been an Indian woman. She was clothed in a kind of textile that we had never seen before; it was very finely woven, and although it was now a yellow color and crumbled to the touch, it had obviously been very rich. About her waist she wore a red sash, and on her feet were black slippers embroidered in gold wire.

We accepted her mysterious presence and her lunar beauty as a miracle, but without too much excitement, since this is, as everyone knows, a land where anything is possible and everything has happened at one time or another. We made her a saint, like Don Salvador, and we made a groove at the front of her tomb so that the door could be slid aside, with the idea that our women could pray to her for their beauty and for that of their daughters, that it might last forever. We called her Nuestra Señora de la Hermosura, and it seemed reasonable to include her in our history as the favorite wife of Don Salvador.

But my brother Manolito was never the same man again. I was with him when he first saw her, and I remember vividly how strange his reaction was. He was a dark man, but he turned pale. He caught his breath, and he told me later that truly his heart ceased to beat for a second or two, so greatly did it leap in his chest. He looked at me with a wild expression, and then made a kind of expansive gesture, as though he were showing me into a richly appointed apartment. "Fíjate," he said, inviting me to look, as though I had not already seen.

"She is very beautiful," I said, but he looked at me again as though I were stupid. "She is exquisite," he replied; it was the first time I had ever heard him use a word as poetic as *exquisita*, and I laughed at him. "Don't fall in love with a corpse," I said, "she will be very boring in bed."

Manolito seemed to take the comment seriously. He put

his hands together, as in an attitude of prayer, and said, "She is lovely beyond the dreams of flesh. One could love her in the spirit and be satisfied."

"You are loco," I replied.

From that day forward Manolito used to go and visit her every evening and sit with the women who were praying to her for everlasting beauty. Like them he kissed her feet and arranged flowers in her hair, and he would linger on after they had gone, until I would have to come and fetch him away to eat his supper. I would find him sitting before her in the sunset, the red gold of the sky lending the glow of life to the woman's face, and often I would sit awhile and fall with him under the enchantment of that celestial face.

I will describe to you shortly the impression made by that face, but firstly I must tell you why she was so special to Manolito.

I cannot remember a time when he had not held in his mind the image of the lady to which he always referred as "my woman." It must have started when he was about twelve years old. We shared a bed in those days, and we would lie there before going to sleep, listening to the crickets and the owls, and the coughing of the jaguar, and often he would talk about "my woman," describing her to me. He told me how she walked with him after he was asleep, holding his hand, teasing him, play-fighting with him in the fields, kissing him on the cheek before he woke up or went on to another dream. For him, "my woman" took on a reality so powerful that he never took a great interest in any other, not even in Raimunda, who could not get him to marry her even though she went to bed with him and got pregnant on purpose. Naturally I laughed at him and called him a dreamer, but he was sincere in his belief, and one day he told me that he had made love with "my woman" for the first time, and that it had been the most beautiful experience imaginable. "I promised to love her faithfully forever," he told me. "From now on there will be no one else." Naturally, I said that I had heard nothing and seen nothing during the night, and he showed me a bite on his arm that he claimed she had put there in sport. I said, "You bit yourself, brother," and he went to great lengths to prove to me that the imprint in his arm was beyond the reach of his mouth, and anyway the imprint was different from that made by his own teeth. In the end I gave in, just to keep him quiet.

But on subsequent nights I was awakened by him heaving and gasping beside me, moaning endearments, quivering with passion, and generally doing all those things on his own that my parents always did together when they thought that we were not around. It was at that time that I took to slinging a hammock outside under the silk-cotton tree, just to get a night's rest, and it was from that time that people began to notice his perpetual expression of sublime contentment and refer to him as "the angel." As for myself, I doubted his sanity, but I was his brother, and so I accepted him as he was, as a brother should, and I even envied him his nights of ecstasy, since I had never had any such myself, even with a phantom.

Manolito only had to see the corpse once to know that he had not waited and loved in vain. The materiality of "my woman" seemed to him to vindicate what he had always known but had never been able to prove even to himself.

But you should not get the wrong idea and start thinking that he transferred his sexual attentions to a dead body, because that is not what happened at all. He visited the body because it had once been the habitation of "my woman;" he visited it because it made solid the stuff of dreams, as though the dream in itself was too ephemeral, too filmy, too evanescent to take hold of when he was not dreaming it. And at night his passion increased until the whole neighborhood was awakened by the cries of his blissful consummations, and people began to protest to my parents about the ferocious animal noises, so that my brother had to move out and build himself a hut on the edge of the cemetery.

Perhaps you will understand my brother's obsession when I tell you that it was indeed a very perfect corpse. The eyes were closed, but Manolito knew that the eyes were violet. There was a perfection of symmetry in those features. The long black hair, parted in the middle, flowed down either side of her cheeks, reminding me of the way that a stream flows when seen from a high mountain, in the gentle curves of nature. The fact that her eyes were closed accentuated her appearance of preternatural peace and tranquillity, of the utmost repose, as though she were alive and in contemplation of something supremely happy. Her eyebrows had obviously never been plucked in vanity, and yet they arched like rainbows that spring from the nothingness of the empty sky. At the upper tip they tapered so finely that one could not say precisely where they finished, and at the bridge of the nose they were full and dark, reminding me of the silky fur of a fine black cat.

Her nose was straight, with the skin stretched so finely upon it that it had the quality that one perceives when looking through the body of a candle held up against a bright light. Her cheeks were a little shrunken in death, which served to lend an extra curve to the formation of her cheekbones. Manolito told me that in reality her cheeks are quite full and that you cannot discern the lines of the cheekbones at all, but in her tomb it gave her the appearance of noble blood and gentle education.

Perhaps it was her mouth that made a prisoner of my brother. It was the mouth of an innocent, and yet of one who knew all the carnality of a sensual woman in the prime of desire. The lips were closed, and yet they seemed to be at the point of opening, as though tempting one to a kiss. There was amusement playing about those lips, betrayed by the two tiny laughing lines at either end. It was the kind of amusement of one who knows a harmless secret; it made one want to say, "Okay what's up? What are you hiding behind your back? Is it a present, or are you going to put a spider down my shirt when you think I am not looking?" It was a very sweet smile.

Because of that ineffable face I can remember next to nothing about the rest of the corpse. The face had a way of fixing your gaze in the expectation of being able to discern some subtle change of mood or the passing of a thought. I think that she had a ring with a large lilac stone on one hand, and I remember that the line of her body seemed as graceful and liquid as the flow of her hair upon her shoulders. All I can say is that she was so lovable that not only I, but also everyone in the village, thought of Manolito's passion as understandable.

But if you want to see her now you will be disappointed. She lives only in the memory of those who are now old, such as myself, because the fact is that the mountain swallowed her up.

We all believed that the mountain was dead, and in fact it was during the generation of my great-great-grandfather that the people stopped giving gifts to the mountain in order to calm its irascibility. It seemed that it was a god who had no longer any appetite for sacrifice or for activity, and even when it finally came back to life it did it with such gentleness that none of us felt terror or fell upon our knees to plead with the illogical Christian God or with the *orishas*. Of course Don José was rushing about in a frenzy. He was shouting "Behold, I am against thee, O destroying mountain, saith the Lord, which destroyest all the earth; and I will stretch out my hand upon thee, and roll thee down from the rocks, and will make thee a burnt mountain. And they shall not take of thee a stone for a corner, nor a stone for foundations, but thou shalt be desolate forever . . ." Don José was very pleased that the cemetery was being consumed because he disapproved of the intercession of Don Salvador and Nuestra Señora de la Hermosura. In fact he once wrote in paint on Our Lady's tomb, "Mystery, Babylon the Great, The Mother of Harlots and Abominations of the Earth." Don José disapproved of female beauty, and he knew all the most depressing bits of the Bible by heart. But the rest of us just stood and watched from a safe distance, without any sense of mortal danger, until suddenly I remembered Manolito. The lava was flowing not down towards the village but down towards the cemetery.

I confess that I did not run and arrive half dead with breathlessness and apprehension. I strolled over, knowing that Manolito had more sense than to lie in his hammock with molten rock lapping at the doorposts. I went just to check that he had made good his escape, and found him watching the spectacle safely to one side and fanning his face with his sombrero. "Ay, brother," he said, "It is all going to one side, and our dead are safe. It is quite something, is it not?"

Unfortunately at that moment there was a kind of belching and gulping noise, and a new fissure opened in the rocks above the cemetery. With consternation in our faces we watched the magma squeeze like dung out of its imprisonment, curving and solidifying, hissing and steaming, and we both had the same thought.

"I will rescue Don Salvador," I said, "and you must rescue Nuestra Señora." I ran to the tomb and slid the stone away in a desperate burst of strength, and I carried the saint away in my arms with time to spare even to go back and fetch one of the hands that had dropped off and the lower half of the left leg as well. I was very pleased and was congratulating myself when I saw that Manolito was still struggling with the slab of the tomb of his beloved. I was about to rush and help him when I saw that I could never make it there before I was consumed in the advancing furnace of golden flame. All I could do was shout above the rumbling of the entrails of the earth, and watch my brother perish.

Manolito did not run. The slab gave way at last, and I saw him size up his chances at the last second. He did what I would have done under the circumstances; he stepped inside the tomb and drew the slab after him, hoping that the lava would pass him by and that he would be protected by the stone sepulchre. If he cried out, I could not hear it above the groans and cracks of the rocks.

I have often thought about the poetic manner of his death. He died in the arms of the woman he had always loved, attempting to save her. He died before age had diminished him, and he died in a fire as incandescent and overwhelming as his own passion. If he cried out in that inferno I would like to imagine that it would have been the same kind of cry that he used to make at night in the embrace of his woman.

We made him a saint, we have many songs about him now, and around here we refer to a lover as a *manolito* or a *manolita*, much as in Costa Rica they refer to youngsters as *románticos*. I go often to show the young people the place where my brother and his beloved embrace so deep beneath the rock, and I never fail to say that if they want to know the way that her hair fell down about her face, they have only to look at the beautiful curves that the lava made as it flowed and set above the cemetery where our ancestors slept.

Carl Phillips

Of That City, the Heart

You lived here once. City—remember?—
of formerly your own, of the forever beloved,
of the dead,

          for some part of you, this part,
is dead, you have said so, and it is fitting:
a city of monuments, monuments to what is

gone, leaving us with our human need always
to impose on memory a body language, some
shape that holds.

              I can picture you walking
this canal, this park, this predictably steep
gorge through which predictably runs a river,

in which river, earlier today, I saw stranded
a bent hubcap, spent condoms, a cup by
someone crushed, said *enough* to, tossed . . .

City in which—what happened? or did not
happen? what chance (of limbs, of spoils)
escaped you?

           And yet . . . I have sometimes
imagined you nowhere happier than here, in
that time before me.

              I can even, from what
little you have told me, imagine your first
coming here, trouble ahead but still far,

you innocent—of disappointment, still
clean. In those historical years preceding
the sufferings

            of Christ, there were cities
whose precincts no one could enter unclean,
be their stains those of murder, defilement

of the wrong body, or at what was holy some
outrage. There were rituals for cleaning;
behind them, unshakeable laws, or—

they seemed so . . . But this city is not
ancient. And it is late inside a century
in which clean and unclean,

                      less and less,
figure. At this hour of sun, in clubs of
light, in broad beams failing, I do not

stop it: I love you. Let us finally, undaunted, slow, with the slowness that a
jaded ease engenders, together

                    step into
—this hour, this sun: city of trumpets,
noteless now; of tracks whose end is here.

Four Poems by Kathleen Peirce

Confession 10.8.13

Collect and recollect. These things I do
within, where, present with me is the world
and whatever I could think of it,
and what I have forgotten. Some things
I buried, though they seemed self-buried,
or slipped out of my mind when they had
glided further into me as I believed
them gone. Once my mouth had been aroused
by the side of a man's thumb moving over it,
the image fixed in me by that impress
recalls the hand, or my heightening,
as if I know my lover when I have him,
or when I have no one. In this way
my mind contains my body and can keep
in mind delight, whether I revisit with the
pleasure of my body, or I revisit thinking
my sad thoughts, or I keep back my desire
like the broken animals.

Confession 11.23.29

My mouth brings loss to me
as it takes measurement of being,
as I think how far, how deep,
how many, how much more,
drawing sentience in always as a double inhalation
of the known and what there might be to expect.
A mirror pressed against a mirror makes

a locked infinity, a bliss ruined by entering,
an anti-kiss. When my mouth opens
against another human mouth,
I measure whirlings of an object on a wheel
which stops (whether or not I pause,
or if I am slow, or quick with love, or twice as quick).
And then I speak of time, and time,
and times, and times, and come to know
loss, so vehemently kindled toward
love, and the mouth of love
which draws away from me.

Nude Against the Light

You for whom the day was sad, among you
there were some whose days are never
otherwise. Among them, there were very few
whose presence shone despair so violent
we hated them. They said
the angels at the feeder are dying as they sing,
they said a painting demonstrates failure to see
the portion of a woman not created with brush strokes,
regardless of the brightness of the room. The room
is bright. So much so that, broken down, the light,
having passed through lace, cut there
by the order of a loveliness particular
and rare, magnifies the objects of the room,
brings them to supplication, to being as a rendering
of surfaces the eye is helpless to resist, there being
so much pleasure in that place. The figure's nakedness is
    drawn
to be included as a surface but resists, as she is other than
a wovenness, a carved thing, painted thing. She was not
made by hand. Neither is she only made of how or where
she looks, as sunshine seems to be. She

regards herself. Or she's already gone, diffused, already
    entered
the seizure of daylight on coverlet and wall, taken by a heaven
of negligible outlines. If this is so, the figure separate
    from light
must be our memory of her. She was so sad, who found
    each pleasure
better than herself and irresistible.

Mountain Laurel

The women were the room and the room was full,
not of women but of cadences and bedclothes, cadences
    irregular
and full, as drapery rounded by a recurrence of a wind
or by sequential unrelated winds all of a night
and of bedclothes, of nightgowns, white bedclothes gone
    blue,
moved on by a wind, rumpled there by bodies, wind,
and night in a long generation of arrivals of nighttime,
and the nightgowns were long also, also repeated, also
blue, and the bodies of the women of the room were loose
and long and white where they had been assigned to sleep,
but they are not sleeping, they will not sleep as they have been
assigned, these several women from the South and elderly.

John McKernan

Room Service

The entrance to the Computer Lab opens like the oak doors to a suite in the Plaza.

Vast threads of CD-ROM talk spiral around the white columns of fluorescent air humming the invisible tune of the tiny fans.

The ceiling glows in the artificial light of 32-bit colors streaming at quadruple speed on a neon nanometer surfboard.

The gift baskets are stuffed with apples and the icons glow on the walls before the flickering vigil lights.

"Yes please. As soon as possible. I'm so hungry I feel that I am going crazy. A large carafe of silence and a tray with several sheets of blank paper."

"O and a knife. A very sharp knife."

Five Poems by Stephen Sandy

Among Bikers

He bestrode each gleaming chopper on the floor;
A kind old man, T-shirted, gave advice.
He wanted a bike his friends could not ignore
And learned how many cc's would suffice,
He found a beauty, and his heart grew sore,
The salesman said, If you must ask the price
You are not ready for a Harley yet;
For that, don't question going into debt.

Malcolm thought money but a spume that played
Upon the heart's own paradigm of things.
Sacking his chauffeur, the great fortune made,
He took off tweed and linen, earned his wings
And dreamed how golden-thighed Knievel rode
Into the burning air, imaginings
A bar made real when he, in leather clad,
Could cruise the dark and feel himself a lad.

Both sons and fathers worship images
But those society approves aren't those
That animate a grown-up's reveries,
But keep a leather or a chrome repose.
And yet they too break balls—O fetishes
That passion, lust, or simple prurience knows
And that all perks of status symbolize—
O little men who mock his macho enterprise!

Biking is celebration, tripping where
No one gets hurt when he knows how to ride
And satisfaction out of the rushing air
Is beauty throbbing. No one ever died

A better death than with the power there
Between his legs, warm cylinders of pride.
No one can ever tell you what it's like.
How can we know the biker from the bike?

For Julia with a Jar of Lupines

Bring me a hank of roses, friend,
Before the garden stiffens.

He had an alert sense of his own need
For material comforts and recognition.

In many ways none of this mattered
But the wine, the important feeling of texture.

Under the lavender foam of cirrus, swallows
Looped; beyond trees, the pavement whined.

Against the heavy cream of enamel woodwork,
Like a bat, the politics of abandon circled.

Garden Wall

But what could they have meant, the old days so small
They looked about to disappear? You heard
They were actually used, although from here they open
To the view like rooms of a doll's house: you'll love it,
Thinking what work it took to get daily
Groceries. Quotidian broils who are you,

Masonry, what's your message?—A lummox in chenille,
A lad in silk; some bags in petticoats,

If they wore smallclothes we wouldn't know. Still
Those five-star days are ours to hold—though they're
Not good for anything and we can't read
The writing, words that are at last just trim

On bric-a-brac. What for example is this one
Saying? We can only make out "full moon,"
And "time," then, on the other side, "autumn."
And isn't that "heart" on the bottom? It all reads like
A legend running around the lip of desire
Overflowing with apprehensions, funky

Musings. Where do they seep to, down there on the floor?
Natural beauties make him sneeze. He looks
Over the edge, gets really close, then weeps
A little, kneeling; tears at the edge of the bed.
Not halcyon days again, credences
Singing everywhere, blooming with fields

Of lavender and purple loosestrife! Then time
For the most important drill, time to go
Back inside and think of the difficult
And what it says, inscriptions written in such
A beautiful hand—and yet so difficult
Almost impossible to make out.

Falling Asleep over James Schuyler

I was home early, had
this beef with someone awful
at the office. No one was home.
The dog had gone on a day trip;
a note said V had gone off
visiting her brother in Sharon.
I went out back, unfolded

my Taiwan lounge with the blue
tubing that sagged; lay back
in some maple shade and started
to catch up on James Schuyler,
which was encouraging. Yes,
for a man who writes about
loneliness so much
his poems are full of people.
Friends at least, if not
faithful lovers. Someone
is always calling, or being
remembered for having called.
Soon I was dropping off,

easy enough to do
on Wednesday at three, more likely
closer to four, perhaps
from being bushed then maybe
just strategic withdrawal
from stress, the trivial little
wants of everyday life.
I felt drops, fat raindrops,
splat on my chinos and
I lurched inside. By the time
I came to my senses, I heard
downpour drumming outside.
Bygorry, I'd left the book
out there. No doubt it was
soaked to its spine by now
but out I ran in the storm,
scooped Schuyler from the grass.
Inside I dried him off
with a towel and fanned the pages
by the fireplace although

I knew such proximity
to a source of sometime heat

was meaningless at this point
in a damp midsummer. I thought,
you knew how to deal with your
isolation and turn it
to solitude—with your
Zen-like dedication to
those spotless details. How strong
and flawless the resignation
became; how sweet, I guess,
that hard fulfillment was.
Now when I open your book
the edges are rippled. That rain
had pinched and crimped the pages
like a pie crust; the little waves
were permanent—mild ruffles
firmly set—when I read them,
flaky now, crackling faintly,
dry like an excellent pie crust.

Diva

Her voice was like a bearded iris in full career
or possibly an Asian lily somewhat blown,
a tall one, but she sang *Delilah* well;
she could stand up to the Philistines or Placido like anything.
Her arpeggios were a breeze, her voice
was roomy and agile in the higher ranges
like a lady smoking as she gives orders to her staff lined up
in her mauve dining room, their mistress by the sideboard
where a silver garniture holds some of those bearded irises
freshly cut and with their leaves spearing in chevrons of *v*s
like foliage in a Rousseau painting shooting up, reeds parting
to reveal a feline, playful but leonine—only
here it is bearded irises with a little stubble
from the calyx at the head of petals, little furls

of short hairs half congealed with scent
as if spoor about to trail along the breeze—

and yet, and yet her voice was like a woman's when
in shade she turns from the Coke machine
in the office hallway at ten past 4 P.M. to address
her lover, one of the bosses, in careless whispers
whose high octaves can be heard all through the office
and echo even off the buildings opposite the windows,
the light of deep afternoon falling across them
and turning tacky, dun vernacular walk-ups
into glowing facades of possible Alhambras rich
in the salmon oranges of teatime sunlight, the
gilt frosting of window panes gleaming gold above
the far-off muted horns of taxis below

that blend & even now harmonize with the liquid
soprano divagations of the diva's sweltering
hover over perfect, then possibly not quite perfect,
pitch, and in the climactic orgy of derision—put-down
party to rag poor Samson—Delilah's voice goes emerald now
among the general citrons and sulphurs of the chorus,
posse half into standing back, a backing off
as the lady of simulations, the lady of the hour,
sits down her loggia from her dogs
and slowly lifts the cloisonné; container, cigarette box,
while turning her smile in the shadow of her hair
toward the adoring boy who only knows her
as Mrs. Warmee; knows her voice, the awning
that fans his day, the limelight, her high spike heels.

Wayne Koestenbaum

Splinters

1. The Origin of Woe

This afternoon I met my woe,
   a formless sound.
I couldn't figure out her sex.
   Fearing my woe would run away

I shouted "Wait!" But my woe
   was out of earshot—
a malingering figure
   hunched on the horizon.

Undaunted by disease,
   I fell to my knees
and prayed. Bells clanged, and my woe
   returned, sweaty with fever.

I took a handkerchief and wiped the wetness.
   "Thank you," said my woe.
I swayed in the seastorm. Tied
   to the mast, I watched clouds scud

pitilessly across the blue.
   Salt air curled my hair.
The subway roared. I exercised
   a fantastic detachment and wore a reversible cape.

2. Telephone, My Mother's Ankle

I telephone my mother's left ankle
   this autumn morning

again. Everyone has a reflection:
  I find myself in conversation

with her left ankle, matching mine.
  You can't already know
the sound of a ringing telephone
  echoes my mother's left ankle.

I must have been an awful infant.
  In sunlight I see
the truth of my iniquity and telephone
  my mother's ankle.

3. Roses Anciennes

The Jews lost faith in me.
  They never had much.
Ancient rose hauntings
  used to be stronger.

We who engage in documentary
  are often tired.
The man in the next world
  paints his walls

with a feather. The walls
  of his body on the fringe
of San Jose in 1970 near the underpass
  have gone away only momentarily.

4. The Mother's Shard

No matter who you are, you open
  your heart to disappointment
when you touch a shard.
  Which? The mother's.

I have no shard at the moment.
 I want to wear
a V-neck sweater and never
 fondle shards.

5. Neurasthenia

Normal, I live beside an ugly church
 and a vendor of fruit juice—
guava, mango. This is an ode
 to serenity. In the end

I doubt I'll call this anarchy
 my own. On the river,
reflected rooftops apologize,
 fearing persecution.

Are they palaces of sin? I thrive
 on denigrated
domino days, Monday knocking Sunday
 onto Saturday.

6. Claustrophobia

I stand on the cusp
 of a giant undertaking.
Now I shall collapse on the floor.
 A twitching bird

dangles below my window.
 Of its import
I'm uncertain. I see
 a Deco stair?

I meant to go beyond the pale,
 and yet I'm still
well within its vast,
 staggered understatement.

7. Transparent Flip-flops

I swam amid turtles in a pool.
   My arms brushed
kelp. On my feet, transparent flip-flops
   battled buoyancy.

My sister's absence and the clouds above
   the violins and court jesters
were forms of usury I could ignore
   until I left the wet

agora. I thank my lust
   for turning
away from cobalt immortelles,
   if they exist.

Aphrodite, lover of young boys
   and grapes, what
early hours I keep, though I was once
   your customer.

8. Redwood Fence Splinter

Peony, aster, or withered carnation
   catapults me back to the redwood fence
splinter era: wandering down unsunny streets
   on Monday past the prime

I recognize Isaac in a natty gray pinstriped suit
   as my master. I have
no master now. No servants, either.
   I still burn myrrh

at shrines, out of habit, not necessity,
   not the root
drive I dramatized to the dense
   derelict nation.

Susan Mitchell

Autobiography

Who am I who speaks to you?

Though that's not it exactly. Try this. What behind
the eyes had looked out so central, so
solid was no longer
in its sours and saccharines, its careful
modulations, not even

a shadow of its   For a long time I watched

the unbraiding into thinner and thinnest   the way clouds
tall stalks of something in a field through which wind
the tassles untassling

I was behind where I stood and up ahead looking back.

Though that's not it exactly.

And how did I feel about all this? I said
that is not the question most likely
to succeed, but even so I'll take it the way

male and female are conveniences, rough categories, the
  make-do.

Is precision a better way? As soon as they asked me
which was more enjoyable I lost the taste
of myself. Though to call who I am
Tiresias would limit
the story. It was as if the one

talking were now a handful of crystals
absorbing the rays of the sun, a spectrum
out there in space, all the colors of the rainbow
primal and urgent, tensed, arched over

and also looking down into a stream
where flowed and wavered the reds, the yellows, green

I don't want to get lost in explaining. The colors
were doing what I was, a correlative
for anger, joy, fear, wonder, eagerness and more, all the
   emotions

so I could look at them, taking my time, naming each one.

And that was it, folks.

Anonymous as hundreds of girls at an air show.

Think flicker and fluid and flow, and all of it
seething and reaching out for
attention the way serpents coupling and uncoupling and

no particular reason why one at any given moment
reigns supreme, all of it up
for grabs, so to speak. Oh, did I forget to say

there was no enclosure, no frame?

I was placed in understanding, and from looking

so long inside, as if at the sun, I was
blinded and had to grope at
my body to know for sure, man or woman

and the shock: was this splitting or growing, adding
or subtracting? I yearned open and where
branch had been, declivity, cleft   as if

pulled inside out by desire.

Is it wholeness I want?

Or fission? Frisson of, its
frequency, its pitch?

Portfolio

Six Dogs

Alan Loehle

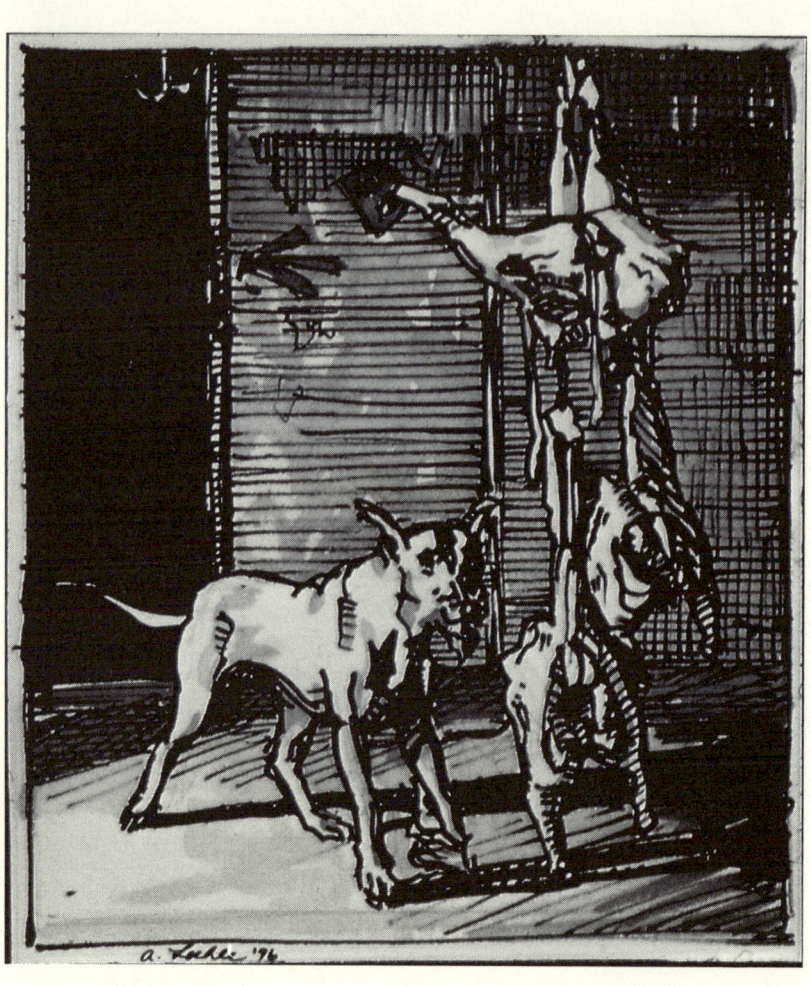

Jerusalem

Simon Armitage

As the vine tree among the trees of the forest, which I have given to the fire for fuel, so will I give the inhabitants of Jerusalem. —Ezekiel 15:6

Title Sequence

Early morning in the Calder Valley, a fingernail moon still hanging in on its hook, the sky growing lighter. A heavy fog in the depressions of the moorland landscape, like thick white smoke.

In the distance, a yellow pickup van motors along a single-track road and disappears into a hollow of mist. Silence, and then the van is upon us, bursting up through the cloud and sweeping along the winding road.

A few quick, jerky images from inside the cab of the van: "The Ride of the Valkyries" playing at full tilt; a mouth below a handlebar mustache singing along, drowned out by the music; one hand on the wheel, the other conducting the

JERUSALEM

orchestra; a pair of big wide-open eyes under a pelmet of heavy eyebrows, fixed on the road ahead.

Outside, seen from a distance, the van comes to a stop above a dark and narrow valley. Seen from behind, a tall man gets out, and with the engine still running walks to the edge and looks down over the canopy of trees. Mist hangs in the air; chimney pots, aerials and satellite dishes poke out curiously above the treetops.

The camera begins a descent of the steep, wooded slope. The first solid houses come into view, clinging to the gradient, improbably two stories high at the front, maybe six or seven at the back, with ingenious pulley systems for hanging out washing or exercising pets, and elaborate chutes for rubbish disposal.

An attic room with a bare lightbulb reveals a New Age couple funneling a large vat of liquid into small bottles. A textile mill converted into units reveals further signs of peculiar nocturnal entrepreneurship. Through one window, a glamour-photography session is in progress—a flashgun discloses naked flesh wrapped in a leopard-skin rug—then darkness again. Through another, a large man in overalls sits asleep, inches away from an ancient, clattering printing press.

Further down, the trees clear to reveal the small and tidy premises of the Jerusalem fire station, complete with a three-hole putting green on the lawn in front and a telephone hatch in the wall. The camera goes in close to the telephone, pauses a moment, then follows the telephone cable down the wall and along the path to the gate of the fire station, where it plunges below ground and burrows its way across the street. We see worms, bones, coins, before emerging on the other side of the road with the cable and shooting up the wall of the Video Kabin opposite.

The cable takes a sharp right past Sugget & Sugget Gentlemen's Outfitters and The Pearl of India (Curry Yorkshire Puddings—Our Speciality) before looping itself elegantly on homemade telegraph poles in front of an unmanned railway station festooned with hanging baskets.

It resumes progress past parking meters and the indistinguishable shopfronts of the Jerusalem Museum of Labor and Craft, and Conroy's General Hardware Store (est. 1882). Then it dives underground again, emerging after another journey through Jerusalem's unsung archaeological past in the taproom of The Hare and Hounds. On the windowsill there's a telephone. In the background, stretched out on a full-length snooker table, lies a sleeping fireman.

This peaceful scene is disturbed by the sound of an engine. Reflected in the taproom window, the yellow van trundles by at a more sedate pace. Inside the van, Wagner still blares, the same eyes observing Jerusalem's shopkeepers opening up for another day.

The shutters roll up on the butcher's to reveal a man in a bloodstained apron reaching inside a suspended carcass for his store of sausages, blood puddings and a float of money.

Through the tobacconist's window an elderly man dressed in jacket and tie weighs out loose tobacco.

At Jerusalem's secondhand-car showroom, a shabby man disappears inside carrying a sack with a woolly leg sticking out of it.

The van turns a corner into a terraced residential street. At the corner shop, Mr. and Mrs. Boot stand motionless side by side behind the counter, hands tucked under their aprons, waiting for the first customer of the day.

Halfway down the street the van stops. Wagner is silenced and the tall, well-built man gets out and unlocks the door of number 27. He returns to the van and throws open the back doors to reveal a clutter of furniture and tea chests.

Across the road at number 28 a curtain on the top floor twitches.

From his bedroom window, John Edward Castle balefully surveys the arrival of Jerusalem's newest resident. Downstairs, peering from behind the nets, Rose Castle's heart beats faster . . .

Who's Who in Jerusalem

John Edward Castle, known as JE, is a man who enjoys power and influence, both in his own home and in the town.

JERUSALEM

JE was a former stationmaster in the local fire service, but an accident at work left him incapacitated and housebound. The accident came about as a result of his near-suicidal bravery and heroism, looking for a child in a burning barn on Bonfire Night twenty-three years ago. From his bed, JE exerts control over his family, friends and acquaintances, and struggles to maintain his status, dignity and self-respect among the good people of the parish.

It's easy to feel sorry for JE because of his disability and his predicament, but his resourcefulness and ingenuity can take on the force of ruthlessness and corruption. His suggestions carry the weight of threats, and those who cross him are quick to be paid back in kind.

Communication is central to JE's regime. With the help of his sidekick, Softie, he uses every available gadget and gizmo to take his voice and his views into other houses, other lives. Trapped in the upstairs quarters of his tall and narrow terraced house, he "talks" to the rest of the family through a tannoy system, with a loudspeaker placed strategically and symbolically on the mantelpiece in the front room, above a roaring fire and beneath a portrait of the man himself in full fire-service uniform, complete with medals.

JE's tentacles extend into the homes of Jerusalem's other residents via a ramshackle, homemade crystal-set-cum-transmitting-device from which he broadcasts regularly to those willing to tune in. His opening gambit is always some cliché from the folklore of broadcasting, from "Testing, Testing, One, Two, Three," to "Attention All Shipping, Attention All Shipping," and even "Germany calling, this is Germany calling." On Saturday nights, JE excels himself, running a bingo session over the airwaves, calling out the numbers in the true spirit of the game, with the compliant Softie, equipped with mobile phone, out checking cards and delivering prizes on his moped. It's JE's dream to be elected Entertainments Secretary at Jerusalem Social Club, and to call out the numbers direct to the club by telephone linkup every weekend.

Balding, bespectacled, slightly flabby and usually sweating,

JE is to be found propped up in bed in blue pajamas, or rattling around his bedroom in a motorized wheelchair, dressing gown and slippers.

Spoon, Jerusalem's ex-police inspector, returns to his old patch after the recent death of his wife, looking to put down anchor. Spoon and JE know each other of old. They lived in the same street, were in the same year at school. Quite simply, they detest each other.

Spoon was a hard man. His reappearance in Jerusalem opens old wounds. It was Spoon that pulled JE from the fire twenty-odd years ago ("Get that bleeding idiot out of there—messing up my paperwork"), striding into the flames in his police hat and shirtsleeves as the fire brigade looked on in oxygen masks and steamed-up goggles. Then in a perfunctory visit to the burns unit in Leeds (to rub salt in the wound, and gloat about his commendation) he found the woman he'd been waiting to meet all his life. It was John Edward's wife, Rose. Over cups of stewed tea in the hospital café they fell in love. Spoon was transformed. His newfound feelings made him generous and expansive, even happy. But when Rose herself became ill with the worry and the guilt, for the first time in his life, Spoon performed an unselfish act. Realizing that Rose would be happier without him despite their love, he packed his bags and left Jerusalem. Six months later he married Janet, a quiet girl from the records department in Halifax. Spoon had settled for a life of romantic disappointment.

It wasn't an ecstatic marriage, but a pleasant and decent one nevertheless, and when Janet passed away before her time, Spoon fell into a long, lonely period of sadness and self-pity. Six years went by, and when the grief subsided a little he found himself looking back across the years to the other love of his life. Now that his days were endless and empty he fell more and more to thinking about Rose. On a whim he drove to Jerusalem, saw that the house opposite was up for sale, and bought it.

The people of Jerusalem find that Spoon has mellowed

over time; maybe there is a cavity of charm and a chamber of warmth, trapped like air bubbles in that solid-steel heart. He's a subtle and sophisticated character, a smooth operator, a gentleman at times in his efforts to win over the hearts and minds of the local population, or the local electorate as they become. But there remains a darker, more sinister side to his personality. He is forceful and persuasive, always one step ahead, never appearing ruffled or wrong-footed. He's a man who looks like he can get whatever he wants, whenever he wants it, a man with a strange and powerful presence. Even the strongest begin to see things Spoon's way after half an hour or so in the man's company.

Six-foot-odd and powerfully built, Spoon is always well turned out in a worsted suit, white shirt, waistcoat and tie, complete with a fob watch on a heavy gold chain. Habitually he produces the watch, flips the catch, notes the time and slips it back in his waistcoat pocket, all in one smooth action. He also enjoys a pinch of snuff, tipping the powder into a hollow at the base of his thumb before snorting it right to the back of his head, nostrils flaring, eyes open wide.

Rose Buckley was the prettiest girl in Jerusalem. She had her pick of husbands, and to this day she can't understand why she chose JE; he was a bully when she married him and hasn't altered much since. In those days she was an optimist, and thought she could bring to the fore the kind and caring man she could see somewhere inside him. But her early married years before the accident were a bitter letdown. She grew to hate JE's regime of tyranny, and was on the point of leaving him when misfortune threw them together forever.

Spoon's friendship and support became important—a lifeline. She could tell him how she really felt and he seemed to understand. To her surprise, delight and horror, she was falling in love. But Spoon left town on the early morning train, and after the birth of her son, Wesley, she buckled down to life with JE. The husband she'd come to despise was now totally dependent on her. She built up a small business, flogging pet food and animal feedstuff to families no less strange than her own. She'd found a measure of independence, if it was only humping sacks of pony nuts and cereal around the slippery pavements of Jerusalem.

Rose oversees an unsteady truce in the Castle home. She tries to maintain the equilibrium of the house but her life is dominated by JE's domestic needs. She manages a number of roles: wife, nursemaid and housekeeper, and keeper of the peace between the embittered JE and her son. Behind closed doors, family life at the Castles' goes on under the foul-mouthed machine-gun invective of JE's microphone, a contrast with the smooth tones of his "public announcement" voice.

Rose is knocked sideways when she looks out of the window and sees Spoon letting himself into the house across the road. Not only is she surprised to see him, but she's astonished by the feelings she'd forgotten she had, feelings under lock and key, tidied away in a box somewhere under the stairs, feelings that were never meant to see the light of day again.

She's a good-looking woman, Rose, but without the time or inclination to do anything about it. She puts on a bit of lipstick to go out shopping. Once a month she treats herself to a perm, coming home with a plastic rain hood over her head, but two hours later her hair is plastered to her head with running up and down stairs, plumping her husband's pillows, wiping the sweat from his brow and the foam from his mouth.

Wesley Castle is twenty-three and works for the Water Board. Water is his element, and all of his spare time is spent fishing—in the river, the canal, the reservoir—anywhere. He's reluctantly joined the local volunteer fire service, with some heavy encouragement from his father. His lack of enthusiasm for the job and his fear of the tasks involved have made for numerous humiliations and a handful of disciplinary proceedings, much to the shame and fury of his father, whose bravery and loyalty to the cause were legendary. Wesley just doesn't look the part: too much like his mum. The homoerotic initiation ceremonies and endless practical jokes leave him ill at ease. He'd rather be fishing.

In every department Wesley is a failure, and JE is never slow to point out the differences between them. "Call yourself a bloody fireman," taunts JE through the tannoy, "you couldn't put out a candle." Wesley finds his tongue, answering back, even if it is on the floor below and out of earshot of the microphone. "I'll murder that bastard, you see if I don't," he says to himself one night, looking up from a textbook towards the bedroom above him. He's studying psychology at night school, and he's just discovered Freud.

Slim, dark, potentially good-looking but not careful about his appearance, Wesley's wardrobe doesn't extend much beyond jeans, T-shirts and trainers, and an old leather jacket when he goes out. He wears glasses to read with. His hair could do with combing, or cutting, or both.

Softie is JE's link with the outside world, his eyes and his ears. He's a small man, wiry and self-contained. At times he appears subordinate and obedient, and seems to have no purpose other than maintaining the growing needs of JE. At other times he's content with his own company, a curious and likeable character, to be found in his workshop, tinkering with some new device, rattling through cryptic crosswords, entering every competition under the sun and quite often winning.

Five-foot-nothing and bald as a billiard ball, Softie is never happier than when he's up to his elbows in electrical cables or engine grease. The pockets of his NCB donkey jacket are stuffed with pliers, spanners, screwdrivers and the like.

Gert, JE's mother, lives next door. Through several years of being left to her own devices she's become eccentric in the extreme. Her house is full of fire-service memorabilia, inherited from her late husband, also a leading fireman. The house is populated with livestock, including geese and a donkey which roams freely from room to room. She's probably the only person able to exercise any degree of power over JE, and watching her, it isn't difficult to imagine where JE's vicious streak came from. "Quack bloody quack," she says to nobody in particular, filling in her bingo card as her son announces, "Two little ducks, twenty-two," on the radio. Rose avoids her like the plague; Wesley slides under her windowsill when he passes the house.

It's hard to say how old Gert is, exactly. She wears her hair piled up above her head, a flea-bitten fur coat at all times, and slips on a pair of seven-hole Doc Martens to go into town.

Wearing identical brown smocks, him with a pencil behind his ear and her with a roll of Sellotape for a bracelet, the Boots stand together behind the counter of their corner shop like Siamese twins, performing an age-old double act for their customers. Unlikely objects are bought, sold and bartered, including the most unappetizing organs of animals and birds. It reflects a sort of self-sufficiency and isolation that hangs over Jerusalem and its residents, like a bad smell that hasn't cleared. Their conversation never goes far beyond two practiced responses. "Thanking you," says George Boot, handing over a slab of meat to a regular customer. "Thanking you kindly indeed," adds Edna Boot as she rings up the price on the till and holds out her hand for the money.

The Story So Far

While JE is observing the unloading of Spoon's van from the bedroom window, the telephone rings, and Alwin Wagstaff announces his retirement as Entertainments Secretary of Jerusalem Social Club at the end of the month. JE senses the opportunity of a lifetime. He could call out the bingo numbers over a public-address system wired from his bedroom, oversee events on closed-circuit television, and generally conduct proceedings from the comfort of his own home. The position would put him right back in the heart of Jerusalem, where he belongs, as well as bringing him the power and influence he craves and the respect he deserves. He switches on the transmitter to make known his intention to stand for election.

As he reaches the end of his address he sees Spoon locking

his van and crossing the street to their house. "Don't let that bastard in," he bellows down the stairs, but it's too late. Rose is mortified and embarrassed by JE's rudeness, and by the confusion of her own feelings as Spoon steps gingerly across the threshold. "I've come to see how you are . . . you know . . . " he says hesitatingly. "I'm sorry, I'm just going out," says Rose, hauling a sack of oatmeal over her back and setting off down the street.

JE broadcasts daily to the electorate of the social club, confident of victory. It looks like being a one-horse race—nobody wants to compete against a man confined to his bed through an act of historic bravery. "You've got to take your hat off to a man like that. Poor bugger."

Rose resists Spoon's attempts to get to know her again. She fears his reappearance could overturn the fragile balance in the Castle household.

Thwarted at number 28, Spoon also finds it difficult to reestablish himself in the town. Everyone remembers Inspector Spoon for different reasons; there are those who respect him and those who are frightened or suspicious. But he's determined to make a name for himself. When he finds out that JE is dragging his name through the mud on the airwaves, spreading gossip and lies, the germ of an idea begins to multiply. "Kill a few birds with the one stone," he mumbles to himself, as he fly-posts the first election poster of his campaign on the lamppost opposite JE's window. Like Uncle Sam, Spoon's finger points from the picture, stretching out to the residents of Jerusalem above the date of the ballot: November 5.

When JE hears of Spoon's plan to fight the election, he goes into orbit. He determines to drive Spoon out of town. The battle is drawn, nothing short of total annihilation will satisfy. As well as a public spectacle complete with manifestos, opinion polls, promises, persuasion, smear tactics, dirty tricks and bribery, the election campaign is a private and personal dogfight between the two of them—a chance to settle old scores and to sort things out once and for all.

As the campaign hots up, JE makes full use of his ever-willing and undemonstrative sidekick, Softie, employing him to plaster the walls of the town with his picture, and leaflet or buttonhole every member of the club. JE's tactic is to butter everyone up, and Softie has his work cut out for him, delivering fresh flowers and homegrown vegetables to all those identified as floating voters. JE's bedroom becomes a Campaign Headquarters, with graphs on the wall charting public opinion, and JE addressing the electorate over the air, making impassioned speeches with *Jerusalem* or *Land of Hope and Glory* blaring in the background.

Spoon's campaigning is more targeted, more calculated. His house calls are short and sweet; quick, clean and clever, and almost always conclude with the promise of a vote. Everyone seems to owe Spoon a favor, and those that don't are the subjects of certain information—dossiers and photographs accumulated by Spoon during his police days, information that Spoon might be willing to let go or lose or forget about—for a price.

On his way back from a house call to an outlying voter, Spoon comes across Rose's van upside down in a ditch, dog biscuits and birdseed scattered across the road. He shouts to Rose inside the car, and is distraught to receive no answer. He jumps down into the ditch and tries to wrench open the passenger door. He is crying, shouting, beating at the window with his fists. From across the road, bruised and dishevelled and half-hidden by a hedge, Rose watches in amazement. Her expression softens. As Spoon lifts a rock above his head to shatter the windscreen, she calls across to him. At that moment a vast flock of pigeons appears from nowhere, circles and swoops down to peck at the seeds. She smiles across at him. For the second time in their lives a near-fatal accident has drawn them together.

Slowly, delicately, their relationship rekindles. Rose is reluctant at first, but eventually Spoon becomes a regular if secret visitor to the house, drinking tea and eating butterfly cakes downstairs while JE bawls orders and requests from his bed in ignorance.

JERUSALEM

Rumors begin to circulate, just as they did all those years ago. They soon get to the ears of Wesley, in whose mind a terrible seed of doubt starts to grow. Counting backwards . . . it couldn't be . . . could it? He wouldn't dream of asking his mother, but his suspicions are further awakened when he returns early from work one day, finding Rose and Spoon sitting close together on the sofa. Rose tries to cover up: "Mr. Spoon was just showing me his flies." And indeed it is true that Spoon has his fishing equipment, including his box of flies, with him in the room. To Wesley there can now be no doubt; a man who shares his passion for fishing and fly tying can surely be none other than his father.

Thrown into turmoil at first, Wesley slowly comes to terms with the idea, and is strangely relieved to think that JE might not be his dad. No need to try and fill the old man's boots anymore; do your own thing, be your own man.

Wesley wants to find out more about Spoon. Early one morning he follows him to the canal and sets up twenty yards away. Spoon eyes him warily—is he about to be confronted about his feelings for Rose? Unsure how to strike up a conversation, Wesley lets his line drift downstream until his float becomes entangled with Spoon's; they begin to talk. There is a wise-owl quality to Spoon that emerges occasionally, a sort of guru-like presence. He explains to Wesley the paradox of fishing: namely, that the best fish lie in the deepest water, but to get anywhere near them means disturbing the surface, and so frightening away the fish. He equates this to life, saying that true peace is always invaded by the person who finds it, and therefore lost. He is full of such nuts of wisdom, and his ruminations appeal to Wesley's thoughtful and introspective nature. Their conversations on the towpath become a regular thing.

From his vantage point in a bird-hide across the river, Softie witnesses these meetings and reports back to a hurt and furious JE. All his attempts to get any closer to his son end in disaster, the more so now that Wesley no longer feels the bonds of loyalty between them. On one occasion, JE summons Wesley to his bedroom in an effort to mend their differences and to do something fatherly. He hands Wesley a shoe box containing all of JE's fire-service medals and his own father's before him, telling Wesley that these are his inheritance, asking him to take care of them. Polished like the family silver, the medals gleam in the light. Embarrassed and uncomfortable, Wesley shuffles out of the bedroom leaving behind a bundle of books from Halifax library. JE begins inspecting the books, whose titles include *The Emergency Services—A Marxist Approach* and *Pump or Penis? Feminist Interpretations of Fire Fighting* edited by Angela Dabydeen. JE goes ballistic, cursing each one. Wesley walks out of the house as the books fly from the bedroom window and crash down around him in the street.

In quieter moments, JE sits in his blankets running Super 8 cine films against the bedroom wall. He watches flickering images of Rose as his beautiful young wife, laughing and throwing snowballs in the park, then scenes of Wesley as a child, on the beach, building sand castles and eating ice cream. Wesley runs towards the camera and turns it on JE, hunched in his wheelchair, trying to cover the lens with his hand. As the film streams past, JE gazes at the wall, silently, tears rolling down his cheeks.

As the campaign continues, Spoon coerces the Boots into his camp by suggesting they might not relish a visit from the health and hygiene people, and by threatening to reveal their illegal offal-smuggling business. "Thanking you . . . Thanking you kindly indeed," say the Boots as they slide a packet of sausages across the counter to Spoon. Back home Spoon takes one sniff of the sausages and tosses them into the bin.

Alwin Wagstaff, the outgoing Entertainments Secretary, is supposed to remain neutral in his overseeing of the election, but his relationship with Gert, JE's mother, calls his objectivity into question. He has been seen on a number of occasions leaving her house late at night by the back door, often dishevelled and flustered, and on one evening wearing what appeared to be a studded dog collar and handcuffs.

A public debate is held between the two candidates, at the club. JE attends in the shape and form of a television, loudspeaker and microphone contraption, rigged up and operated by the diligent and dexterous Softie. At the other end of the platform, Spoon is smartly dressed, well-informed, and charming.

(*A packed house at Jerusalem Social Club, all seats taken.* ALWIN WAGSTAFF *is center stage, dressed in a dickey-bow and tuxedo, puffing on an enormous cigar. To his right,* SPOON *stands behind a lectern with his arms crossed in front of him, impeccably groomed, dressed in a dark suit and tie. To* WAGSTAFF's *left, an ancient television encased in a mahogany cabinet flickers on top of two in-turned chairs, with a loudspeaker at either side and a microphone craning over the top towards the audience.*)

WAGSTAFF (*Clearing his throat*): Ladies and gentlemen, best of order if you please. We all know why we're here, so let's get on with it. I'm sure neither candidate needs introducing, but I'll introduce them in any case, beginning with Mr. Spoon on my right.
SPOON: Good evening.
WAGSTAFF: And on my left, er, in spirit if not in body, Mr. John Edward Castle. Can you hear me, JE?

(*Silence. The TV continues to flicker.*)

WAGSTAFF: JE, can you hear me?
NEVILLE SHACKLETON (*From the back of the hall, with a pint in his hand hr*): Ground control to Major Tom.

(*Much laughter in the hall.*)

WAGSTAFF: Best of order, please.
NEVILLE SHACKLETON: Is there anybody out there?

DONALD STONEWOOD (*Also from the back of the hall, also with a pint in his hand*): One small step for man, one giant leap for mankind.

(*The back of the hall erupts with laughter.*)

WAGSTAFF: Best of order, please. Can anybody sort this thing out?

(SOFTIE *leaps on to the stage from his seat in the front row, and begins adjusting the horizontal hold on the television until a picture of JE's face emerges, obviously in the bedroom of his house, spruced up and with his hair slicked back, wearing a patch of tissue on a shaving cut and adjusting his tie.*)

SOFTIE: We've started, JE. Lift off. You're on the air.
JE (*Ruffled, and looking down at his notes*): Oh, er, er, good evening everybody. (*He continues, reading from a script.*) Friends, family and acquaintances, I'd like to begin by thanking you for giving up your valuable time this evening to come and see things as they really are.
WAGSTAFF: Yes, thanks JE. Now, if I could . . .
JE: (*Cutting across him*): It's my opinion, and one which I share with all right-minded people of this town, that the position of Entertainments Secretary is a position of honor and responsibility . . .
WAGSTAFF: Thank you, JE. I really do feel that we should be . . .
JE (*Carrying on regardless*): And with this in mind I've put my own name forward, as a man who's lived and breathed Jerusalem since the day he was born, and not some fly-by-night, here one minute and gone the next . . .

(*Wesley slides down in his seat. Rose covers her face with her hand.*)

WAGSTAFF: JE, I really think we should . . .
GERT (*Intervening*): Oh shut up, for God's sake, JE, or we'll be here 'til bloody midnight.

(JE *becomes silent.*)

ROSE (*to Wesley*): I can't bear it. I'm going.
WESLEY (*taking hold of her hand and pulling her back into her seat*): Come on, Mum. Give him a chance.
WAGSTAFF: Thank you, JE. And thank you, Gert.

(GERT *winks at* WAGSTAFF, *who blushes and almost loses his cigar.*)

WAGSTAFF: Without further ado, then, does anyone have any questions?

(*Almost everyone in the hall raises an arm.* WAGSTAFF *picks out* COLIN BUTTERWORTH *at the back.*)

COLIN BUTTERWORTH (*Being egged on by his pals*): Wor about doffers?
WAGSTAFF: I beg your pardon?
COLIN BUTTERWORTH: Wor about doffers? Strippers?
WAGSTAFF: What about them?
COLIN BUTTERWORTH: Well, will we have 'em, or won't we?
WAGSTAFF: I see. I'll put that question to Mr. Castle first. JE, as I understand it the question is as follows: should you be elected, would you be inviting strippers to come and . . . er . . . perform at the club?
JE: Well, as far as I'm concerned it's just a bit of harmless fun, isn't it?

(*Someone at the back shouts "speak up a bit."* SOFTIE *stands up and adjusts a knob connected to the TV by a long length of cable. The word* volume *appears across* JE's *face, along with a set of red dots that increase from left to right.*)

JE: Always has been, always will.
NOREEN KNOWLES (*Standing up in the middle of the hall, shouting*): It's a disgrace.

(*Lots of agreement amongst the women.*)

JE (*Flustered, trying to keep on top of the situation*): It's not something I'd be interested in personally, obviously, but it's

traditional, isn't it? And if somebody wants to get their kit off on stage, she can do, and those who want to watch can watch, and those who don't want to don't have to. Yes. Thank you.
ROSE (*Under her breath*): Nude women? He'd run a mile.
WESLEY: Aye, if he could.

(ROSE *slaps* WESLEY *on the knee but has to smile at the same time.*)

NOREEN KNOWLES (*Standing again*): It's a disgrace, that's what I say.

PAULINE MUMP: I agree.
WAGSTAFF: Thank you everybody. Best of order, please.
COLIN BUTTERWORTH: Wor about you, Spoon? Are we goin' to have strippers or not?
SPOON (*Taking his time*): Male or female, Mr. Butterworth? Which are you interested in?

(*There is a great roar of laughter, especially from the back of the hall.* COLIN BUTTERWORTH *goes red and sits down.*)

SPOON (*Self-assured, speaking clearly and confidently*): In my view, it's the feeling of the membership that counts, not just the opinion of one man. After all, we don't want to hurt anybody's feelings. But I will say this: Jerusalem Social Club has a reputation second to none, and a waiting list that reflects that reputation. I should also say that we shouldn't ask anyone to do anything that we wouldn't be prepared to do ourselves, so I suggest we think long and hard about this one, unless of course Mr. Butterworth wants to come up here and show us what he had in mind.

(*Uproar and cheers in the hall. There is general agreement, and a lot of nodding of heads.*)

WAGSTAFF: Lewis Pike, your question please.
LEWIS PIKE (*Standing, and reading from the back of an envelope*): I'd like to ask Mr. Spoon and Mr. Castle about their qualifications for the job, relevant experience and so on, and

the sorts of entertainment we can expect to see at the club, bearing in mind the excellent standard set by Mr. Wagstaff over previous years.
WAGSTAFF: Very kind of you to say so, Lewis, very kind.
LEWIS PIKE (*Standing again to reply*): Pleasure, Alwin.
WAGSTAFF: Mr. Spoon?
SPOON: During the years I've been away from Jerusalem, I built up a successful chauffeur and escort service—looking after some very big names, making arrangements for tours, hospitality and such like, and I can tell you that I made some very important contacts along the way. As proof of this, I'd like to offer this letter, just as a taste of things to come.

(SPOON *takes a letter from his inside breast pocket, and hands it to* WAGSTAFF. WAGSTAFF *puts on his glasses, unfolds the letter and reads from it.*)

WAGSTAFF: "My dear Mr. Spoon. Just a short note to thank you for all your endless patience and dedicated professionalism, and for making my tour a very smooth and successful one. If I can ever repay the favor, please don't hesitate to ask. Yours affectionately, Shirley . . ." (*To* SPOON): I can't quite make out the signature.
SPOON: Bassey, I think you'll find. Shirley Bassey.

(*Uproar again in the hall. Lots of excitement.*)

SPOON (*Producing a whole wad of letters bound in a red ribbon*): And there are plenty more where that came from.
GERT (*Standing up*): It's bollocks. Tell him, John.
JE (*Gob-smacked*): I don't believe it.
WAGSTAFF (*Smelling the letter*): Perfumed as well.

(ROSE *bites her lip, hiding her feelings.*)

WESLEY (*To himself*): Unbelievable.
GERT: It's rubbish. All rubbish. Tell him, John.
JE (*Complying with his mother's instruction, losing his cool*): Oh very smart, Spoon, very smart. But don't think we don't know what's going on. Don't think we can't see right through

you. You think you can come here with your fancy talk and fancy letters, and pull the wool over everybody's eyes, don't you?

WESLEY (*To himself*): Here we go.

(JE *bangs the camera with his head, and carries on talking with only half of his face in frame.*)

JE: Well let me tell you, you've got it wrong. All wrong. This isn't the London Palladium, and I don't care if you've got promises from Elvis Presley or Jesus bloody Christ for that matter, because they're not needed.

ROSE (*Standing up*): John, will you calm down? You'll make yourself poorly.

GERT: Let him talk, woman.

JE: Tradition, that's what this club's built on. Bingo Friday and Saturday night, a singer or comic from Leeds or Bradford, Manchester even every now and again, the odd Country and Western night, discos, race trips, raffles, a bit of supper . . . It's that kind of thing that makes this club what it is, and that's what people want. Am I right, everybody? You tell him, you tell him that's what you want.

(*There is silence in the hall.*)

NOREEN KNOWLES (*Standing, to* SPOON): Have you really met Shirley Bassey?

SPOON: Well, I . . .

JE (*Irate now, out of breath and in a real lather*): Has he bloody hell as like. And what do we care if he has? What do we care if he's met Shirley MacLaine or Shirley bloody Williams. We don't need 'em. Shirley Bassey my arse. Who's he going to bring up next? Tom Jones?

SPOON: Actually, it's funny that you should mention Tom, because it was only last week . . .

(*There is a crackle of electricity and* JE's *TV goes dead.*)

NOREEN KNOWLES: If he can get Tom Jones, he's good enough for me!

JERUSALEM 125

(*The club erupts again at the prospect of Tom Jones.* GERT *gets up from her seat in a fury.*)

GERT: Have you no respect? For a man who gave the best years of his life and both his legs for this town?

(*Shouts of "Sit down, you old bat." * GERT *throws her pint tankard towards the direction of the shout. Chaos breaks out. Another glass flies towards the front of the room.* WAGSTAFF *bangs his gavel.*)

There is almost a riot in the hall. Rose turns on Spoon and snaps at him for belittling JE in public, then runs home to her husband to save him from embarrassing her and humiliating himself further. Spoon follows her back to the house, and arriving there finds the door open but no answer. He can hear voices so he goes inside, to the kitchen, and over the tannoy he hears Rose and JE upstairs, JE hysterical with rage. JE rants on about Spoon, accusing Rose of unfaithfulness all those years ago. Evidently it is an argument they have rehearsed many, many times over; the cadences of Rose's weary protests sound as well-worn as JE's raving accusations. Eventually JE's anger turns to tears. Rose tries to comfort him. Spoon sits in the kitchen, downstairs, listening to JE demoralized and sobbing, and Rose's voice whispering, "There, there, it's all right now, come on, it'll be all right."

Bonfire Night—the night of the election. The whole of Jerusalem is illuminated with the biggest bonfire imaginable and alive with the snap, crackle and pop of fireworks. Members drift into the club all evening to cast their votes, and are greeted on the doorstep by Spoon, who gives everyone a very firm handshake and a straight look. At the other end of town, Wesley attends a fire at an old farmhouse. Fire crackles inside, smoke pours out of every window, and it looks as if the roof is about to collapse. Wesley puts on the breathing equipment with instructions to go in. Terrified, he enters the house with the blaze reflecting on his visor and images of JE's accident flashing in front of his eyes. Rigid with fear, a trickle of urine runs out over his boots. Just when it looks as if he might faint he is pulled out of the fire by a colleague. Spitting with venom and calling him a chickenshit coward, the chief officer punches him in the face, calls him a disgrace to the uniform and sends him home.

Back in bed, JE goes wild when Wesley brings him the news, telling him he has brought shame on the family. Their full-scale war of words culminates in Wesley tearing the tannoy from the mantelpiece, throwing it into a cupboard and slamming the door, JE's voice still raging like a man trapped in a coffin. JE, or rather the tannoy, is rescued by Rose, as Wesley storms out of the house and into the pub.

Rose leaves the house to go and cast her vote, and meets Spoon standing on the steps of the club. Rose becomes tearful, telling him she doesn't know what to do for the best. Spoon puts his arm around her, tells her to follow her heart. A rocket goes up into the sky and explodes, lighting them for a split second like the flash of a camera.

Towards the end of the evening, Spoon goes into the club and asks "which way the wind is blowing." Elsie Conroy, speaking out of turn, tells him that as things stand the election is a dead heat, with only himself and Wesley still to vote. Spoon goes back onto the steps and lights a cigarette.

Suddenly, Wesley arrives in a drunken rage, cursing JE, saying that he'll vote against him, out of sheer spite. "That'll show the old bastard, won't it?" On the other hand, if he lost, life in the Castle house wouldn't be worth living—especially for his mother. Spoon tells him not to be too hard on JE—it can't be easy being cooped up in a bedroom all day. Can't be easy, trying to be a father in that state. Plucking up courage, Wesley asks, "Ever have children yourself, then?"

"No," replies Spoon. "Plumbing problem."

Spoon tells Wesley that it's too late to vote, because the poll is closed. Demoralized and defeated in every way, Wesley wanders off into the night, a loser once again, and a failure. Spoon extinguishes his cigarette by grinding it into the ground, goes into the club and casts the final vote.

Elsie Conroy picks up the telephone. We follow the cable underground, then up and over and across the houses and telegraph poles of Jerusalem and in through the bedroom window of the Castle house. The telephone rings. Elsie Conroy informs JE that by the margin of a single vote he is the new Entertainments Secretary of Jerusalem Social Club. It's official. JE goes straight to his broadcasting equipment and begins transmitting the news. He is jubilant, triumphant, ecstatic, victorious, unbearable. He delivers a pre-prepared acceptance speech full of excessive promises and thanks to all his loyal supporters. He even manages, magnanimously, to find a kind word for his beaten opponent, Spoon, but speculates that a man with any pride would have to leave town with his tail between his legs after such a humiliating defeat. His broadcast continues over the following scenes.

Gert leans towards the bedside table, turns on the radio and listens to her son proclaiming the good news. She lifts a pint of tea from the Teasmade and settles herself in bed. On the pillow next to her are a pair of feet. At the bottom end of the bed, Alwin Wagstaff's face emerges. He hears the result, looks around the room and pulls the covers back over his face.

The Boots stand behind the counter of their shop as they listen to JE's voice on the radio. Mr. Boot crosses himself as he hears the result. "Thanking you, Mrs. Boot." "Thanking you kindly indeed, Mr. Boot." Mrs. Boot bends to the pile of newspapers and kindling in the hearth and puts a light to it. Outside, a plume of white smoke rises from the chimney.

In the secondhand-car showroom, Spoon's van sits under a handwritten sign: BARGAIN OF THE WEEK. ONE CAREFUL OWNER. In Spoon's back garden, a pile of furniture and clothes is burning in a small bonfire, unattended.

Bleepers go off in the homes of several volunteer firemen, and the telephone rings in the snug of the Hare and Hounds.

Firemen race towards the station and fling open the doors, only to find the fire engine vanished into thin air. They stand around, scratching their heads.

Somewhere on the shore of a Scottish loch in the early morning mist we discover the said fire engine, its turntable ladder fully extended out over the lake, with Wesley sat on the last rung, fishing from the deepest water, undisturbed. He hauls out another trout and drops it into the bucket which swings from the ladder.

Softie walks down Jerusalem's main street, tearing down the election posters and ramming the shredded paper into a bin bag.

As JE's speech soars, we see Spoon walking out on to the empty platform of Jerusalem railway station with his suitcase, wearing the same clothes he arrived in. He takes a pinch of snuff. He checks his fob watch, and with one fluent movement slips it back in his pocket. A minute later, Rose emerges behind him on the platform, also carrying a suitcase. They stand about ten feet apart, aware of each other's presence, but not acknowledging it. The train arrives, obscuring our view from the other side of the line, and when it pulls out the platform is empty.

JE's commentary has now reached the heights of a church sermon. Looking out over the town, the remains of the bonfire are still smouldering in the valley bottom as the train disappears into the tunnel.

THE END

The Sniper's Story

J. David Stevens

There's a hill east of the village, not as tall as others, but I can see every road worth seeing. Someone planted tulips around a maple up there. I don't know why—maybe a family buried a dead pet, an orange tabby cat perhaps. You know, they eat their animals now. I've seen old women through my scope trailing after dogs, holding cleavers or boards with nails behind their backs.

But the hill. The tulips smell best in late spring, and I often bring a book to read. I used to excel in school. This year alone I have read Twain, Stendhal, Borges and Joyce. My father just sent copies of Proust and Mann. The translations are good ones, I think, but soon I hope to study in France and read the originals myself.

I am still surprised watching people die. When shot, they fall the same way, folding in air like acrobats then flattening quickly against the pavement. Sometimes the wounded will try to drag themselves to an alleyway or a door. I can't explain why I finish off some wounded but not others, any more than I can explain why I don't shoot the lovers into whose window I can see. They make love promptly at three each afternoon, suggesting characters out of Hugo or Flaubert.

My mother found God last year and tells me to pray. In the brush below me, I can see our troops move without caution; the village does not have enough ammunition to mount an attack. Sometimes I train my rifle on the backs of men I know. I imagine shooting one or two, just to remind them how random things are.

When the wind blows off the mountains, I close my eyes, inhale the flowers and picture the beginning of time. I set my fingertips against the smooth rifle stock and think about maples, solid and tall, grown like bayonets or excited lovers all the way to the end of the earth.

Anthony Hecht

Le Jet d'Eau

after Baudelaire

My dear, your lids are weary;
Lower them, rest your eyes—
As though some languid pleasure
Wrought on you by surprise.
The tattling courtyard fountain
Repeats this night's excess
In fervent, ceaseless tremors
Of murmur and caress.

> A spray of petaled brilliance
>   That uprears
> In gladness as the Moon-
>   Goddess appears
> Falls like an opulent glistening
>   Of tears.

Even thus, your soul's arousal,
Primed by the body's joys,
Ascends in quenchless cravings
To vast, enchanted skies,
And then brims over, dying
In swoons, faint and inert,
And drains to the silent, waiting
Dark basin of my heart.

> A spray of petaled brilliance
>   That uprears
> In gladness as the Moon-
>   Goddess appears
> Falls like an opulent glistening
>   Of tears.

You, whom the night makes radiant,
How amorous to lie, spent,
Against your breasts and listen
To the fountain's soft lament.
O Moon, melodious waters,
Wind-haunted trees in leaf,
Your melancholy mirrors
My ardors and their grief.

 A spray of petaled brilliance
  That uprears
In gladness as the Moon-
  Goddess appears
Falls like an opulent glistening
  Of tears.

Bin Ramke

A Great Noise the World Makes

Ardea Candidissima, snowy
Heron or White
Egret, printed London 1835, not
the Great White, evil-
eyed with savaged prey in beak, but
the one with the hunter,
tiny figure, slipping forward
from the background. Figure/ground
:to the privileged eye

the bird appears to see us, ("See
how it follows you
around the room")
(I'll make a quick story:
the bluecoated figure
topping the rise halfway
between the verandahed tiny
house and the yellow-
footed bird, a distance
of seven inches, is Audubon
himself, gun in hand intending
to study, abetted by
the distracting audience.)

Of the white birds he drew
this one whitest,
something Chinese in the
composition. The sky
on this edge of America
is jungled air
along the bayous; the boil

of insects rises as the sun
sets, the night random
with nesting birds
which test the darkness from time
to time, would raise a small ruckus.

I collected feathers, kept
the herons' in a ginger jar
though they were broken, cast
off for good reason. We called all
such birds cranes and watched
with no purpose their constant crossings
the dangling *Y*s of legs,
their sleek *S* necks and
the soft incised *W*s in the mud.
Is there a difference between speaking
and not speaking?
Between sound and

silence in other words?
A past determined so severely
the present that he could not wait?
Someone gazing softly
into the hard distance would know
to avoid this kind of attending,
this Nature. *Natural*
being our word for *necessary*.
Like killing time. Inserting
wires through the fresh corpse's
limberest parts—especially the neck,

the machined armature turns
beast into pliant mimesis.
Don't you just love anyone
who wants everything,
or at least one of each kind? Any
collector, say. Life-list

long as your arm. He wanted
to draw every kind of bird
in America. Noah
merely followed orders, but this
Frenchman suffered, walked
to New Orleans from Kentucky,
drew portraits of Creoles then tutored
their children for money. Meanwhile

drew birds and birds and birds.
Lovely little landscapes
beneath their craning necks,
for instance,
or sometimes small dramas,
a Laocoön of nestlings and snake.
The flat land of watercolor
teeming with rubrication and
all sorts of imitation, shimmer
and sheen. A thing to make,
a book of birds flattened, paper
covered with ink, printed and bound,
darkened with covers and collation.
It was never quiet
there, among the streaks
and daubs. Always they spoke
to him; no, but
screeched and squawked and screamed.

Few noises made by birds,
real or imagined, can be
called music. Mostly anger and fear,
sometimes lust, induce
the piteous or the terrifying timbre.
A frenzy of desire
collects reversing shadows

and reflections in a dewdrop,
then dries to powder on the page.
The work men do,
and the mending required:
birds rise that way, they fly.

Melanie Hope

Sixth Grade

I knew the dick size of every boy in my grade,
my measure being how it filled my fist
when I squeezed it through their jeans. In return
I let them feel my tits, the biggest in class.
Some girls hadn't graduated to bras, but even they
were squeezing dicks. I, muscled tall and thick,
was known for being rough: boys feared and hoped
I would be the one to conquer their dicks.

Our teacher had a pregnant wife. I would try
to imagine his dick, turning away whenever
my gaze locked with his ambiguous
blue eyes. I remember squeezing dicks
and flaunting tits in sixth grade, thinking
I must be learning something about love.

Two Poems by Stephen McLeod

At the West Street Piers

for José Joaquin Zuleta Colon

Something about what matters
   Breathes in the twilight blushing
      Everything here on the piers.

Latin boys in tanktops,
   Cycle by, winking and whistling.
      You ignore it. You smoke like a pro.

What I love most about
   This city is the light.
      Not only the natural light

Vesting each tenement
   With golden damask, unfolding
      Pumpkin dusks like gowns,

But also the light that salmons
   Busy hearts inside
      Our grown-up lives into children's.

A tourist takes our picture:
   Arms over shoulders like pals,
      Uninjured, unashamed.

In the shot, this crumbling pier
   Blinds like a Turner harbor,
      Light-infused and torched

From inside with *composition*.
  For a generous, frozen moment,
    There is no disease invading,

No shadow in this brief
  Caesura between day
    And the sure, descending night.

The Borgo of the Holy Ghost

The earthly city affords its shrug-of-shoulders luster
simply by being there.
Not avarice not lust nor even pride preserved it.
I set my course toward
The simplest, pinkest light. And if I find myself
in love, for example, or caught
By the unsettling glare of someone's constant attention,
it isn't the point of life.

At the end of a shady tunnel, a waist-high marble plaque
reports, by a straightish line
engraved below the Latin, its cursive script difficult,
the level the Tiber crested
in 1274. Above, a shrine of more
recent vintage: an overturned
glass of flowers singed by a votive recently spent,
itself knocked over.

The better guidebooks will miss, while noting the genre,
such windows as these.
The same flooded year, Aquinas collapsed and found
the long-awaited answer
to questions never asked at Lateran IV, where he
forfeited his seat to Another.
And seven centuries later, you are born while somewhere,
another flood threatens.

Remarking a disaster, or even a rendezvous
with deeper life, it's true,
can signify the sense that some things are important,
especially when they're cut
in the best Italian marble. But everyone has a birthday,
and this, at least, implies
that someone loves you enough to tell you what it is.
We get by on our looks in the end,

by what we've weathered or by what we've allowed.
I can't think of anything better
to hope for than the plowed and planted meadow where
I've cast my seed with yours
and waited for a generous summer. And so I am led to you
by ancient lanes and tunnels,
routes long established for someone else's shortcuts,
prayers and landmarks.

This plaque is not conceivably near today's Lungotevere. Still,
I suppose it's the same river.
And as we emerge, my heart, unhinged, releases its rudder:
Before me, unexpected,
lit by cool fluorescence, the Pantheon looms like the Host
displayed in a dazzling monstrance.
It is Christmas night. The edge of a suddenly antique sky
spills over, accommodating

the pillowy glow that rises from discreetly placed lighting.
I touch with my whole hand
a large, bewildering column pocked like the moon, but solid.
I listen for the sound
Humming beneath my fingers of two thousand years.
I've never touched anything so unmistakable,
nothing stranger. *I forgot to tell you about this*,
you say, inscrutable, smiling.

Two Poems by Sue Kwock Kim

The Korean Community Garden in Queens

In the vacant lot nobody else wanted to rebuild,
dirt scumbled for years with syringes and dead
weed-husks, tire-shreds and smashed beer bottles,
the first green shoots of spring spike through—

bullbrier, redroot, pokeweed, sowthistle,
an uprising of grasses whose only weapons are themselves.
Blades slit through scurf. Spear-tips spit dust
as if thrust from the other side. They spar and glint.

How far can they climb, grappling for light?
Inside I see coils of fern-bracken called *kosari*,
bellflower cuts named *toraji* in the old country.
Knuckles of ginger and mugwort dig upward,

working through soil and woodlice until they break
the surface. Planted by immigrants, they survive,
like their gardeners, though ripped from their
native plot. What is it that they want, driving

toward a foreign sky? How not to mind the end
they'll come to. Imaging the garden underground,
where gingko and ailanthus grub cement rubble.
They tunnel slag for foothold. Wring crumbs of rot

for water. Of shadows, seeds foresung as *Tree
of Heaven* and *Silver Apricot* in ancient Mandarin,
their roots tangle now with plum and weeping willow,
their branches mingling with tamarack and oak.

I love how nothing in these furrows grows unsnarled,
nothing stays unscathed. How last year's fallen stalks,
withered to pith, cleave to this year's crocus bulbs,
each infant knot burred with bits of garbage and tar.

Fist to fist with tulips, glads, selving and unselving
daffodils, they work their metamorphoses in loam
pocked with rust-flints, splinters of rodent-skull—
a ground so mixed, so various that everything's born

of what it is not. Who wouldn't want to flower
like this? Look how strangely they become
themselves, this gnarl of azaleas and roses-of-Sharon,
native to both countries, blooming here as if drunk

with blossoming. Green buds suck and bulge.
Stem-nubs thicken. Sepals swell and crack their cauls.
Lately, every time I walk down this street and peer
through the fence, I'm surprised by something new.

Yesterday hydrangea and chrysanthemums burst
their calyxes, corolla-skins blistering into welts.
Today jonquils slit blue shoots from their sheaths.
Tomorrow daylilies and wild-asters will flame petals,

each incandescent color unlike: indigo, blood, ice,
coral, fire-gold, violet the hue of shaman's robes—
every flower with its unique glint and slant, faithful
to each particular. Each one lit by what it neighbors

but is not, each tint flaring without a human soul,
without human rage at its passing. In the summer
there will be scallions, mung-beans, black sesame,
muskmelons, to be harvested into zinc buckets

and sold at market. How do they live without wanting
to live forever? Unlike their gardeners in the old world,
who die for warring dreams and warring heavens,
who stop at nothing, life the one paradise they wanted.

Monologue for an Onion

I do not mean to make you cry.
I mean nothing, but this has not stopped you
From peeling away my flesh, layer by layer,

The tears clouding your eyes as the table fills
With husks, ripped veils, all the debris of pursuit.
Poor deluded human: you seek my heart.

Things have no hearts. Within each skin of mine
Lies another skin: I am pure onion—pure union
Of outside and in, surface and secret core.

Look at you, cutting and weeping. Idiot.
Is this the way you move through life, your mind
A questing knife, driven by your fantasy of truth,

Of lasting union—slashing away skin after skin
From things, ruin and tears your only signs
Of progress? Enough is enough.

You must not grieve that the world is glimpsed
Through veils. How else should it be seen?
How will you strip away the veil of the eye, the veil

That you are, you who want to grasp the heart
Of things, who long to know where meaning
Lies. Smell what you hold in your hands: onion juice,

Gashed peels, my stinging shreds. You are the one
In pieces. Whatever you meant to love, in meaning to
You changed yourself: you are not who you are,

Your soul severed moment to moment by a blade
Of fresh desire, the floor strewn with abandoned skins.
And at your inmost circle, what? A core that is

Not one. Poor fool, you are divided at the heart,
Lost in its maze of chambers, blood, and love,
A heart that will one day beat you to death.

Scott Coffel

Andrei and Natasha

In a blow to Marxist thought, our romance red-shifted
from farce to tragedy. I had the paper trail to prove it,
a receipt from the erotic bakery with your phone number
and testimonial to the doctrine
of mutually assured orgasm. The Days of Awe were at hand
and I was grateful for something to atone for.
Years and two lovers apart, we kissed good-bye, nostalgic
for the future as rain speckled our trench coats.

The Russian winter came early to New York State.
Though corrupted by property and jealous of your freedom
I accepted your collect call, amalgamating
phone sex with *War and Peace*, my life-thwarted prince
dying in your arms as the Antichrist reached Oneonta,
the City of the Hills where love began and ended.

~~A flowerless funeradia b~~

A flowerless funeral, a blizzard of one blown into view
~~Out~~ From the shadow of domes in the city of domes, and, weightless,
Entered your room, and made its way to an arm of the chair
Where you, looking up from your book, saw it the moment it landed.
That's all there was to it. No more than that, than your
Solemn waking to brevity, to a ~~notion of~~ whiteness ~~passing~~ becoming
~~So~~ shadow, the lifting and falling away of attention, swiftly.
~~Swiftly.~~ A time between times; Then ~~some the~~ feeling ~~came to you~~
That this tiny piece of the storm, which ~~dissolved~~ turned to to nothing,
Before you go, Would come back ~~years hence, because you believed~~ years hence and
~~Out of nowhere~~ that the Warden of Twilight ~~would~~ say:
It ~~was~~ is time, the air ~~was~~ to ready, the sky had an opening.

A snowflake,
~~A flowerless funeral~~, a blizzard of one blown into view
from the shadow of domes in the city of domes, ~~of Parisian air~~,
And, weightless, entered your room, and made its way to the arm
of the chair where you, looking up from your book, saw it the moment
it landed. That's all there was to it. No more than that, than
your solemn waking to brevity, to a flowerless funeral, the lifting
and falling away of attention, to whiteness

No more than a solemn
waking
to brevity, to ~~a flowerless funeral~~, to the lifting and lifting falling away
of attention, swiftly, a time between times, No more than that,
a flowerless funeral

*A manuscript page of "A Piece of the Storm,"
from Strand's most recent book,* A Blizzard of One.

Mark Strand

The Art of Poetry LXXVII

Mark Strand was born in 1934 on Prince Edward Island in Canada. His parents were from the United States. His father did many different things—you could call him a businessman—and his mother was at different times a schoolteacher and an archaeologist. When Strand was an infant, the family lived in Halifax, then Montreal. When he was four years old, they moved to Philadelphia. Attending public school there, Strand at first spoke very little English and had a heavy French accent. "Mocked and generally brutalized by my classmates," Strand learned English fast. But then his father, now working for Pepsi-Cola, took the family to Cuba, Colombia, Peru and Mexico. "I moved around so much, and went to so many different schools, that I never found my own place," Strand has said. "I really come from nowhere. But I was fortunate in that many of my summers were spent on St. Margaret's Bay, near Halifax." During these happy summers, he discovered a landscape "that became internalized," that became "the one I carried with me wherever I went: the sea, the runty pines along the coast, the big lichen-covered boulders, cold mornings . . ."

Although he wrote a little poetry in high school and read and wrote poetry while attending Antioch College, he entered the Yale School of Art and Architecture intending to become a painter. (When he was nineteen he had worked one summer in Mexico as an assistant to David Siqueiros, helping to create "a kind of art I learned to despise while I was working on it.") But, while studying painting, he became an ardent reader of Wallace Stevens, and somewhat to his surprise found himself taking English courses, writing poetry and winning the admiration of some of his English professors. In 1960 he was given a Fulbright Scholarship to Italy to study nineteenth-century Italian poetry. Soon after, some of his own poems began to be published in The New Yorker, *and he began to feel that he was going to devote his life to poetry. His first book of poems,* Sleeping with One Eye Open, *was published by the Stone Wall Press in Iowa City in 1964, and in 1968 Harry Ford took his collection* Reasons for Moving *for Atheneum. Strand says that "I owe my professional career as a poet to Harry Ford."*

During the sixties Strand formed influential friendships with the poets Richard Howard, Charles Simic and Charles Wright. Another friend and poet who played an important role in his life was Joseph Brodsky, whom he met in the seventies.

Strand has published eleven books of poetry, a book of sui generis short stories called Mr. and Mrs. Baby *and a disturbing meditation on immortality in the form of a prose poem,* The Monument. *He is currently teaching at the Committee on Social Thought at the University of Chicago, where this fall he is giving a course on Plato's* Symposium *with the philosopher*

Jonathan Lear. In 1987 he was awarded a MacArthur Fellowship, and in 1990 he was the U.S. Poet Laureate at the Library of Congress. He has also translated the poetry of Rafael Alberti and Carlos Drummond de Andrade and written monographs on the paintings of William Bailey and Edward Hopper.

Strand says that the elements he requires in order to be able to write are "a place, a desk, a familiar room. I need some of my books there. I need quiet. That's about it." Asked if he ever writes in a less tranquil spot, such as on a train, he replies that he does, but usually only prose, because it's "less embarrassing. Who would understand a man of my age writing reams of poetry on a train, if they looked over my shoulder? I would be perceived as an overly emotional person."

He writes in longhand and delays typing for as long as possible, he explains, because "when I read a poem in longhand, I'm hearing it. When I read it in typescript, I'm reading it. A poem can appear finished just because of the cleanness of the typescript, and I don't want it to seem finished before it is. A poem has already been brought into the world to some extent when it's typed. I feel more like an editor than a poet after that." Often, after reading what he has typed, he'll "go back to longhand for a few weeks."

The interviewer has known Strand as a friend for many years. He unabashedly used the interview as an excuse to ask questions about poetry and the life of the poet, which in many cases he had always wanted to ask. It's often hard to ask a friend crude or elementary questions about the field of work to which the friend has devoted a lifetime. Nonetheless the interviewer, who writes for the theater but reads quite a bit of poetry without ever being sure that he really understands any of it or knows what it is, although he knows that he loves Strand's work and always has, plunged ahead with a hard-earned simplemindedness.

The interview took place in a bare, sublet apartment on Greene Street in New York.

WALLACE SHAWN

I started reading that thing that that guy wrote about you. But it upset me, because he kept talking about the themes of your writing, and I didn't get it. I don't think I really get the concept of "themes." So I'm not going to ask you questions like, What is your view of nothingness? because I don't get that, exactly.

MARK STRAND

I don't get it either. And I'm not sure I could articulate a view of nothingness, since nothingness doesn't allow a description of itself. Once you start describing nothingness, you end up with somethingness.

SHAWN

In any case, do we read poetry because we're interested in "themes"? Or do we read it to learn about someone's view of the world? To find out if the poet we're reading sees things the way we do?

STRAND

You don't read poetry for the kind of truth that passes for truth in the workaday world. You don't read a poem to find out how you get to Twenty-fourth Street. You don't read a poem to find the meaning of life. The opposite. I mean, you'd be foolish to. Now, some American poets present the reader with a slice of life, saying, "I went to the store today, and I saw a man, and he looked at me, and I looked at him, and we both knew we were . . . thieves. And aren't we all thieves?" You know, this is extracting from everyday experience a statement about life, or a moral. But there is another type of poetry, in which the poet provides the reader with a surrogate world through which he reads *this* world. Wallace Stevens was the twentieth-century master of this. There's no other poetry that *sounds* like a Wallace Stevens poem. But then, there's nothing that sounds like a Frost poem, either. Or a Hardy poem. These people have created worlds of their own. Their language is so forceful and identifiable that you read them not to verify the meaning or truthfulness of your own experience of the world, but simply because you want to saturate yourself with their particular voices.

SHAWN

Well, your poetry is obviously very much in this category. When we read your poetry, we are enticed by the voice—and then led into a world that you have created. And at first, I would say, we can more or less picture or imagine the scenes you conjure up, although they may consist of elements that in our daily world would never be combined in the way you've combined them. Sometimes, though, in your poems—quite often, really—we reach a point that is almost, one could say, Zeno-like, in which we're asked to imagine things that are either almost self-contradictory or literally unimaginable. I mean, in a surrealist painting, a painter could present a very strange landscape, but he couldn't present one like this! This couldn't be painted!

STRAND

Well, I think what happens at certain points in my poems is that language takes over, and I follow it. It just sounds right. And I trust the implication of what I'm saying, even though I'm not absolutely sure what it *is* that I'm saying. I'm just willing to let it be. Because if I were absolutely sure of whatever it was that I said in my poems, if I were sure, and could verify it and check it out and feel, yes, I've said what I intended, I don't think the poem would be smarter than I am. I think the poem would be, finally, a reducible item. It's this "beyondness," that depth that you reach in a poem, that keeps you returning to it. And you wonder—the poem seemed so natural at the beginning—how did you get where you ended up? What happened? I mean, I like that, I like it in other people's poems when it happens. I like to be mystified. Because it's really that place which is unreachable, or mysterious, at which the poem becomes ours, finally, becomes the possession of the reader. I mean, in the act of figuring it out, of pursuing meaning, the reader is absorbing the poem, even though there's an *absence* in the poem. But he just has to live with that. And eventually, it becomes essential that it exists in the poem, so that something beyond his understanding, or beyond his experience, or something that doesn't quite match up with his experience, becomes more and more his. He comes into possession of a mystery, you know—which is something that we don't allow ourselves in our lives.

SHAWN

We don't?

STRAND

I mean, we live with mystery, but we don't like the feeling. I think we should get used to it. We feel we have to know what things mean, to be on top of this and that. I don't think it's human, you know, to be that competent at life. That attitude is far from poetry.

SHAWN

An experience of total immersion in mystery that I once had was reading the first half of Heidegger's *Being and Time*. You know, it was really totally up to you to sort of create this world in your own head, and whether what was in your head was what was in Heidegger's head—who could possibly guess?

STRAND

Well, when I read poetry I can't imagine that what's in the reader's head is ever what was in the poet's head, because there's usually very little in the poet's head.

SHAWN

You mean . . .

STRAND

I mean, I think the reality of the poem is a very ghostly one. It doesn't try for the kind of concreteness that fiction tries for. It doesn't ask you to imagine a place in detail; it suggests, it suggests, it suggests again. I mean, as *I* write it. William Carlos Williams had other ideas.

SHAWN

But do you suggest something that you yourself have already pictured?

STRAND

I'm picturing it as I'm writing it. I'm putting together what I need to have this thing be alive. But sometimes it's more complete than at other times.

SHAWN

When you say that when you write language takes over, and then you follow it, you're implying that the experience of writing is one in which at least to some extent you're in a passive role. Something is coming to you from somewhere, and you're receiving it. But where is it coming from? Is it just the unconscious? That would be psychoanalysis. It's coming from somewhere else, isn't it? Or . . .

STRAND

I don't know where it comes from. I think some of it comes from the unconscious. Some of it comes from the conscious. Some of it comes from . . . God knows where.

SHAWN

I think the "God knows where" part is quite . . .

STRAND

Poems aren't dreams. They just aren't. It's something else. People who write down their dreams and think they're poems are wrong. They're neither dreams nor poems.

SHAWN

As you write, you're listening for something. But then you at some point take an active role in creating the poem.

STRAND

I get caught up in where it's going because I don't know where it's going. I want to know, I want to push it ahead, a little. I add a few words, and then I say, "Oh no—you're on the wrong track."

SHAWN

But the type of poetry you're describing can be frustrating to the reader. A lot of people I know would have to admit that their basic model for what reading is would be something like the experience of reading *The New York Times*. Each sentence is supposed to match up to a particular slice of reality. If that's a person's expectation about reading, then your poems might be . . .

STRAND

Well, sometimes poems aren't literal representations of anything. Sometimes a poem just exists as something else in the universe that you haven't encountered before. If you want a poem to say what it means, right away, clearly—and of course the poet who writes that kind of poem is usually talking about his or her own experiences—well, what happens when you read that kind of poem is that it puts you back in the world that you know. The poem makes that world seem a little more comfortable, because here is somebody else who has had an experience like yours. But you see, these little anecdotes that we read in these poems and that we like to believe are true, are in fact fictions. They represent a reduction of the real world. There's so much in our experience that we take for granted—we don't need to read poems that help us to take those things even *more* for granted. People like John Ashbery or Stevens do just the opposite—they try to explode those reductions. There's a desire in Ashbery, for example, to create perfect non sequiturs, to continually take us off guard. He creates a world that is fractured. It doesn't imitate reality. But, looking at it from another point of view, you *could* say that it's simply a world that is as fractured and as unpredictable as the world in which we move every day. So there's an element of delight in these people who rearrange reality. We usually hang on to the predictability of our experiences to such an extent . . . and there's nowhere else where one can escape that as thoroughly as one can in certain poets' work. When I read poetry, I want to feel myself suddenly larger . . . in touch with—or at least close to—what I deem magical, astonishing. I want to experience a kind of wonderment. And when you report back to your own daily world after experiencing the strangeness of a world sort of recombined and reordered in the depths of a poet's soul, the world looks fresher somehow. Your daily world has been taken out of context. It has the voice of the poet written all over it, for one thing, but it also seems suddenly more alive—not as routinely there.

SHAWN

Of course, when you talk about poetry in that way, you're going on the assumption that your reader is willing to put quite a bit of effort into following you—in contrast to writing for the theater, for example, where it's more normal for one's colleagues to say, "The people aren't going to get this. Clarify it."

STRAND

I think a poet writes a poem not feeling that he must be understood on the first or second reading. He writes a poem hoping that the poem will be read more than once or twice, and its meaning will be revealed over the course of time, or its meaning will reveal *itself* over the course of time.

SHAWN

When you say you hope that a poem will be read more than once or twice, how many times do you mean? How many times do *you* read a poem?

STRAND

When I write my own poems, I read them hundreds of times to myself. But when I read other people's poems I will read them dozens of times, sometimes more than dozens of times. I don't know why this should seem strange. The average churchgoing person who lives in the Bible Belt will have read the same passages in the Bible hundreds of times, and they will have revealed to him more each time.

SHAWN

An actor in a play goes through a similar process, really, and acting could in a sense be seen as a form of reading, I suppose. The actor goes over the text hundreds of times, seeing more and more implications and different possible meanings inside each individual line, and at the same time seeing *through* the various clichés of interpretation with which he has at first mistakenly overlaid each line.

STRAND

Well, a good reader of poetry may be very much like an actor working on his part, because he reads the poem aloud to himself again and again, and sometimes he learns it by heart. And it becomes familiar. It, finally, becomes part of him.

SHAWN

The actor experiences the play again and again. But the audience member doesn't. Plays are so different from poetry, because they're written on the assumption that everything must be immediately comprehensible.

STRAND

Well, theater is meant to be heard by a large audience and it must communicate many things on that first experience, on that first encounter. A poem releases itself, secretes itself, slowly—almost, sometimes, poisonously—into the mind of the reader. It does it with cadence, it does it with combinations that might strike the reader as beautiful. Of course, God knows what the beautiful is. I don't know. Because the beautiful fifty years from now will be what is seen as the ugly now, or what's insupportable now or barely tolerated now. But, you know, I think if you try too hard to be immediately comprehensible to your audience, if you give too much to the moment, you're also giving too much to the status quo. The poet's obligation isn't to his audience, primarily, but to the language that he hopes he's perpetuating. And when you think of how long it takes us to understand each other, for example—and how much leeway we give other areas of knowledge in our lives—why can't we be a little more patient with poetry?

SHAWN

Maybe the *New York Times* reader just isn't in the right frame of mind to *read* poetry.

STRAND

Well, you can't expect to jump from *The New York Times* into John Ashbery or Jorie Graham. Language is put to a different test. And it's used for different ends. The language of a poem is meant to be meditated on. You clear a psychic space for poetry that's different from the one you clear for prose. It's a space in which words loom large. And this cleansed psychic space that readies itself for a poem is really one in which the poem is both read and *heard*.

SHAWN

But how does a person prepare such a psychic space?

STRAND

Well, if you spend a lot of time alone, particularly if you're thinking about your life, or other people's lives, you're already used to the space I'm talking about. There are certain painters I know to whom the language of poetry means a great deal. And it may be because these people spend a lot of time in front of canvases, alone, with nobody to talk to, that they're prepared: they're ready to take the poem in. Their minds are not full of a lot of noise and clutter and unfulfilled desire. I mean, you have to be willing to *read* poetry; you have to be willing to meet it halfway—because it won't go any further than that if it's any good. A poem has its dignity, after all. I mean, a poem shouldn't beg you to read it; it's pathetic, if that's the case. Some poets fear that they won't be heard unless they flatter the reader, go 90 percent of the way, do it all for the reader. But that's pathetic.

SHAWN

Damn! I'm sort of worried that we're not living in the right world to read what you and the poets you admire are writing.

STRAND

Well, poetry—at least lyric poetry—tries to lead us to relocate ourselves in the self. But everything we want to do these days is an escape from self. People don't want to sit home and think. They want to sit home and watch television. Or they want to go out and have fun. And having fun is not usually meditative. It doesn't have anything to do with reassessing one's experience and finding out who one is or who the other guy is. It has to do with burning energy. When you go to the movies, you're overcome with special effects and monstrous goings-on. Things unfold with a rapidity that's thrilling. You're not given a second to contemplate the previous scene, to meditate on something that's just happened—something else takes its place.

SHAWN

It's strange that we feel we're escaping into a great variety of pleasures, but in fact so often those apparently various pleasures somehow turn out to have a lot in common.

STRAND

We seem to want instant gratification. Violent movies give you instant gratification. And drugs give you instant gratification. Sporting events give you instant gratification. Prostitutes give you instant gratification. This is what we seem to like.

But that which requires effort, that which reveals itself only in the long term, that which demands some learning, patience or skill—and reading is a skill—there's not enough time for that, it seems. We forget that there is a thrill that attends the slower pleasures, pleasures that become increasingly powerful the more time we spend pursuing them.

SHAWN
The activities you mention are all nonverbal ones. Maybe language in general is slowly losing out in some sort of weird competition in the world.

STRAND
Well, but on the other hand, we do talk to one another. And we do read other forms of writing, other than poetry. We would be lonely if we didn't use words. We are dependent on them. We're just dependent on them in a certain way. And that dependency doesn't extend to poetry.

SHAWN
Maybe people avoid poetry because it somehow actively makes them nervous or anxious.

STRAND
They don't want to feel the proximity of the unknown—or the mysterious. It's too deathlike; it's too threatening. It suggests the possibility of loss of control right around the corner.

SHAWN
When you say deathlike . . .

STRAND
Well, when I say the unknown—death is the great unknown. I mean, most lyric poems lead to some acknowledgment of death. In fact, most poems are dark and dreary affairs that have to do with death and dying, or loss of one sort or another—loss of love, loss of friends, loss of life. Most lyric

poems are sad, because if you think deeply at all about your experience, you think about your experience in time—your life—and if you're thinking about your life, you can't avoid the fact that it will end in death. In fact, everything about a poem—the meter of the poem, or the measure of the poem—is a reminder of time. Even a line that's repeated: we're back again. I think that the popularity of villanelles or poems that use refrains, is caused by the fact that they seem to enact a stay against time, they seem to give us a momentary reprieve from what usually is the subject of the poem, or the matter of the poem. So, although the poem may be about dying or death, we have repeated lines that seem to say we haven't really gone anywhere, we're back again. But in the end, that just helps us to hold on to the loss that is in the poem. It helps us to remember it.

SHAWN

In some of your own poems, death is kind of disturbing, but in others, it isn't that bad.

STRAND

It's inevitable. I feel myself inching towards it. So there it is in my poems. And sometimes people will think of me as a kind of gloomy guy. But I don't think of myself as gloomy at all. I say ha ha to death all the time in my poems.

SHAWN

Dr. Dorn in *The Sea Gull* says, "The fear of death is an animal fear. You've got to suppress it."

STRAND

We *are* animals, though. Oh, we can overcome it briefly. It's not always in mind.

SHAWN

Personally, I always think it's *life* that's surprising. Most things are dead, and they always have been. Rocks, water, sand, et cetera. And then, a *squirrel* is born. *We* are born.

Life bubbles up briefly. And then it stops. Why wouldn't it? I mean, that animal fear of death, that I might feel when I wake up in the middle of the night and think I have a terrible illness . . .

STRAND

That's the way life sustains itself.

SHAWN

Yes, it's an evolutionary advantage to have that fear. But *aside* from that rather stupid fear . . .

STRAND

Well, it's a fear of not being there.

SHAWN

I think I'm too dumb to mind.

STRAND

Oh, I don't mind either. But I wouldn't choose to go right now, or tomorrow!

SHAWN

No, no, it would be terribly sad. But I've always been somehow—I mean, as far back as I can remember, my mother would come to me and say, "Wallace, something *terrible* has happened." And I would say, "What *is* it?" And she would say, "Mrs. Grabowsky *died*." And I would just not have any reaction. And it's gone on like that, really, for most of my life. Of course, there are certain people whom you might miss tremendously, because they're not there anymore. But in itself, it seems quite natural to me that, at a certain point, people die.

STRAND

The thing to rejoice in is the fact that one had the good fortune to be born. The odds against being born are astronomical.

SHAWN

Astronomical. You can say that again. I totally agree. But if poetry in a way *is* inherently disturbing and likely to provoke anxiety, is prose any different?

STRAND

Well, I think a poet's focus is not quite what a prose writer's is; it's not entirely on the world outside. It's fixed on that area where the inside meets the outside, where the poet's sensibility meets the weather, meets the street, meets other people, meets what he reads. So a poet describes that point of contact: the self, the edge of the self and the edge of the world. That shadow land between self and reality. Sometimes the focus is tipped slightly in favor of the self, sometimes, more objectively, in favor of the world. And so sometimes, when the balance is tipped towards the self, strange things are said, odd things get into the poem. Because the farther you are from the world that everybody recognizes as the world, the stranger things look. I mean, some novels do this, but most don't. Most novels are focused on what's out there, and the novelist erases himself, by and large, to keep the narration going. There are some narrators who insert themselves, as Philip Roth does brilliantly and amazingly. I'm always dazzled by his books. The world is electrically alive in *American Pastoral*, for example, but he's there, too: Roth is Zuckerman, and he's there, he's telling the story. We're never unaware of the fact that he's doing it, but we're never wholly aware of the fact that he's doing it. In a sense, that book is more magical than any poem I've read recently.

SHAWN

I had no idea you were such a Philip Roth fan. So am I! Do you think of yourself as someone who reads widely, in many different sorts of books? Would you call yourself a person who spends a lot of time reading?

STRAND

I have gone through periods in my life of reading a great deal, and others in which I barely touched a book. There are certain novels I enjoy reading and rereading. There are poets I read and reread. I tend to reread more these days, because I know what I've enjoyed, and I like to go back and see if I enjoy those things in the same way; often it's a gauge on how much I've changed. There was a period at one time when I read Wittgenstein. There was a period when I read the romantic poets, and would read Wordsworth quite a lot. There was never a period in my adult life when I didn't read and reread Wallace Stevens, or Elizabeth Bishop. There's never been a period in my adult life when I haven't derived pleasure from reading Philip Roth or, on the other hand, Samuel Beckett. Or Italo Calvino, or Tommasso Landolfi. Or Bruno Schulz, or Franz Kafka. Great poets like Octavio Paz I've read and reread over the years, Joseph Brodsky, Derek Walcott. There are also younger poets I read with a sense of awe: Jorie Graham, Charles Wright, Charles Simic.

SHAWN

I know that you know your way around quite a few languages—Spanish, Portuguese and Italian, at least—and you've done a certain amount of translating. Has that experience been valuable to you in regard to your own writing?

STRAND

Translating is almost like a game. It is a serious game, because, finally, it's your reading of another poet's work. But you develop a sense of syntactical possibility—you make choices, you have to say to yourself, when you're translating, Should I do it this way, or should I do it that way? When you're writing your own work, you're not asking yourself those questions. Maybe at some much later stage in the writing of a poem, you may say to yourself, objectively, I need a two-syllable word here, with the accent on the first syllable. The line should end here, instead of there. There should be a slant rhyme, some assonance or something here . . . But when you're writing, at the beginning, when you're writing, you're not asking yourself those questions. When you're translating, you always are.

SHAWN

In translating, you're looking at your own language from an unusually analytical point of view, taking it apart and seeing how it works, studying its structure in a practical way. What did you mean when you said that a poet's first responsibility was to the language?

STRAND

Well, in writing poetry, one wants a certain flexibility in the use of language, a flexibility that can keep alive successes in the language from the past, that is, other poems, and that will also insure that whatever poetry comes next will capitalize on the successes instead of on the failures. The fact is that we take many of our cues on how to proceed, and our ideas about what is a good line, or a beautiful line, from what we've experienced from the poetry of the past. In other words, it would be nice to know that poets in the future will have read the best poets of today and yesterday, that they won't simply base their poems on news reports or instruction manuals. You know, so that there's some continuity in the language of poetry. Because it's complicated, but we're defined by the best that's written in our language and so we want to perpetuate the best that's written in our language. If poetry becomes just a revision of the newspaper page or the talking heads on TV, that's not a language that will last; it's not a language that translates into the future.

SHAWN

But then what would you think of a poet, or someone who said he was a poet, a student, let's say, who came to you and said, "Well, I'm only interested in the present. I don't know about the poetry of the past, I don't like it, and I'm not too interested in it"?

STRAND

Well, I would ask him, "What poetry have you read that makes you feel that you want to write poetry?" Because usually what draws us toward poetry is the individual voice that we want to hear—the voice of Wordsworth, the voice of Keats, James Merrill, Anthony Hecht, whoever it is. The chances are that a person who doesn't feel any desire to hear such voices may not turn out to have a very original voice himself.

SHAWN

So you do in a way agree with the academic writers who always seem to imply that the parents of poems are other poems, as opposed to what I'm always wondering, which is why couldn't the greatest influences on a poet be the people he's known, or the experiences he's had every day, rather than the poems he's read?

STRAND

Well, it all depends on the poetry you write. Some people may be more influenced by their mothers and less influenced by Robert Frost. It differs with different poets. But by and large, I think poets are more influenced by other poems than they are by what they eat and whom they talk to—because they read other poems deeply, and sometimes they don't eat dinner deeply or chat with a friend over the telephone deeply. Because poems not only demand patience, they demand a kind of surrender. You must give yourself up to them. Once you've done that, and allowed them to enter into your system, of course they're going to be more influential. This is the real food for a poet: other poems, not meat loaf.

SHAWN

But what about the idea that a poet should be influenced by a wide range of experience, that a poet should explore *life* and allow it to affect him? Don't you have any feeling that you should do everything, at least once?

STRAND

I don't have to try everything on the menu to know what it is that I like. I can make a reasonable guess as to what I *might* like, and so that's what I will order. I don't go out of my way to experience every possible thing, because that's dangerous. I want to protect myself. I want not to experience many, many different things, but to experience the things I choose to experience well, and deeply.

SHAWN
Some writers, for example, have tried to enhance their work by writing under the influence of alcohol or drugs.

STRAND
They interfere. I mean, if I've had a couple of drinks, I don't feel like writing. I feel like having another drink. Or I feel like going to sleep.

SHAWN
But if poems, including poems from the past, are really a poet's main food, doesn't that lead to some rather odd consequences? For example, poets always seem to love to quote other poems in their poetry. I mean—my God—if a contemporary playwright put lines from some nineteenth-century play in one of his own plays, it would be considered, well, ludicrously academic.

STRAND
Well, too much of that can be burdensome or overbearing. But sometimes it's delightful; sometimes there's a perfect line that just fits in your poem, and it comes from a poem that's a hundred years old. Poetry is always building these connections. It's not showing off. It's the verbalization of the internal life of man. And each poet forges a link in the chain, so that it can go on. That may be a grandiose way to think of it, but it's certainly not academic. I mean, academics really know very little about poetry; they experience it from the outside. Some of them are ideal readers, but their job is to make connections. It's the way they read, the way they *have* to read. But why should we allow the reading of an academic to become a paradigm for the way we *all* should read?

SHAWN
Well, but some modern poetry, like *The Waste Land*, has been so full of connections—connections and allusions—that emergency academic help has been required in order to read it.

STRAND
Yes, it would have been impossible for me to have read *The Waste Land* without critical intervention.

SHAWN
But isn't there something wrong with that? Or don't you think so? I mean, you don't write like that.

STRAND
No.

SHAWN
Well, why don't you? Would you write that way if you felt like it—or do you have any objection to that?

STRAND
I don't. I mean, Eliot was a very learned guy and, you know—he wrote a very allusive poetry. My poetry is much more self-contained. I think that there are all kinds of poetry possible—there are all kinds of people possible. *The Waste Land*, the *Cantos* of Pound—this is one kind of poetry. It's a very extreme case of allusiveness. These are men who were intent on revising culture; that found its way into their poetry.

SHAWN
And you're willing to make that journey?

STRAND
Sure!

SHAWN
It's worth it. You don't think it's an outrageous thing to do.

STRAND
No. By what standard would it be outrageous? Only by the standard of how easily one can understand the daily newspaper. But say one's standard were trying to understand what is most difficult and most elusive in ourselves. How do we know who we are, and what we are? How do we know why

we said what we said? If you use that as a standard, then *The Waste Land* becomes simple. Well, less difficult.

SHAWN

The problem is that, because of the importance of very allusive modern poetry, a lot of people, at least in my generation, were given in their school days a sort of screwy idea of what poetry *is*, and it put them off poetry for life. I'm very grateful that I had some wonderful English teachers, because the bad ones did try to teach us that poetry was simply a game, in which you substituted a certain group of words for the code words offered by the poet. When the poet said *water*, you crossed it out and wrote *rebirth*, et cetera. It was all, "This is a symbol of this, this is a symbol of that." And in a certain way, we got to *hate* those symbols.

STRAND

Well, rightfully. It sounds tyrannical on the part of the teacher, to submit you, and to submit the poem, to that. I mean, I don't think teachers who are forced to teach poetry know why they're teaching it, or what poetry provides. Some poems aren't paraphrasable, just as some experiences can't be readily understood—and yet we live with those experiences. I mean, we can *love* a poem and not understand it, I think. There's no reason why we can't live with a poem that doesn't deliver meaning right away—or perhaps ever. You know, somebody should have asked the teacher, "What's the relationship between the meaning of a poem and the *experience* of a poem?"

SHAWN

We didn't *have* an experience!

STRAND

It's as if the paraphrase of the poem was meant to take the place of the poem, and the poem was lost.

SHAWN
I'm afraid so.

STRAND
You know, the idea is to experience the poem! But this is the reversal that takes place: the poem becomes a surrogate for what the teacher has to say about it.

SHAWN
Well, I mean, *literally*, because in my old school books, the physical poem is actually obliterated by the notes I've taken on the teacher's interpretations. The page is a swirl of arrows and circles and scrawled-in words. You could never read the original poem.

STRAND
I don't know why teachers are afraid of the *experience* of the poem . . .

SHAWN
Well, because it would be like passing out drugs in class, I imagine.

STRAND
Poetry *is* a high. It is a thrill. If people were taught to read poetry in the right way, they would find it extremely pleasurable.

SHAWN
It's also an experience of close contact with another mind, another person.

STRAND
Well, certainly something I would want a reader to have as he experiences my poetry is—a form of intimacy.

SHAWN
Yes. But of course—how can I put this—as a reader, I wouldn't want to have that intimacy with everybody.

STRAND

No. You have to like the voice. I mean, you have to like the music you hear.

SHAWN

Right. And it's quite a personal and individual matter what voices you like. It's hard to predict. Like a lot of our other most personal preferences, it goes deep into the individual psyche. I think one of the reasons I was first drawn to your voice—without thinking about it, of course—is that you use very short words, even words that are easy to pronounce and spell. I *like* that. Maybe I'm speaking about something awfully superficial—but it's true, isn't it? For example, a word like *cytoplasm*, which has a weird spelling—am I right that you avoid that sort of word?

STRAND

I avoid those words because I don't use them in conversation either. Scientific words are usually composite Latinate words. I don't favor those; they're finally very abstract—they're really representations of other words. So I favor the immediacy of plain Anglo-Saxon words: monosyllables, you know, two-syllable words. My preference has always been for simple, declarative sentences, simple words. Of course, my poems have become much more elaborate, the sentences . . .

SHAWN

But the words haven't become more elaborate, I don't think.

STRAND

No.

SHAWN

You always seem to be growing and changing as a poet. Have these lifelong predilections ever posed a problem for you as your poetic universe expands?

STRAND

Well, I feel that anything is possible in a poem. But the problem is, as a poet develops, he develops a predisposition to use certain words—which create or suggest certain landscapes, or interiors, or certain attitudes. Those, in fact, become his identity as a poet. So when a subject with a vocabulary he has never used asserts itself, it may be difficult to accomodate. It will seem strange and may eventually be repudiated in favor of the words which he or she knows will work, because finally—despite experimentation and all the self-righteousness attendant on experimentation—it's more of our own poems that we want to write, more of *our own poems*, poems that sound like they were written by us. It's a terrible limitation. I mean, in some ways, this is where John Ashbery's genius is so marked—that he's got such a large vocabulary that it accomodates everything. He can talk about Goebbels, or hummingbirds, steam shovels and hemorrhoids, all in the same poem. And he could do it, probably, within ten lines—and it would sound like Ashbery! But a poet whose vocabulary is very reduced—say, limited to words like *glass, dark, stone*—those were my words for years—couldn't do that. He would conjure up the same bleak landscape, again and again. I felt I had to sort of break through that limitation. And so you have, in my long poem *Dark Harbor*, many other things cropping up. You have Marsyas and the Mafia, the muzhiks being slaughtered, Russian women at a dinner party . . .

SHAWN

Yes. And the length of that poem was itself also a new thing for you. Did you like writing a long poem?

STRAND

Well, there's something relaxing about writing a long poem. You know, you don't have to sharpen the edges quite as much. The focus on a single poem is sometimes overwhelming. It's kind of blurred in a long poem.

SHAWN
And you just sort of fell into those three-line stanzas?

STRAND
Well, I wanted certain controls. Sometimes it's helpful to have a grid, to keep a visual contract. It gives you something to shoot for, and you begin to see that your sections develop a kind of rhythm. I mean, just thematically. Because if you know it's an eight-stanza section, then when you're at stanza seven, you know you're getting towards the end, and you've got to wrap it up! You're thinking about wrapping it up in stanza six.

SHAWN
I think it was Allen Ginsberg who said that after the age of thirty-five he never revised any of his poems. The first draft was the only draft.

STRAND
Some people believe that's the way to write poetry.

SHAWN
Have you ever been interested in trying that approach?

STRAND
Well, I would *like* to write just one draft of a poem and have done with it, but it rarely happens. It's only happened a very few times. You know, I'm not one of the geniuses that gets it right the first time. But there are people who do.

SHAWN
Well, there *may* be. We'll never know—they may secretly be hiding a thousand drafts of their poems. Anyway, who cares? If we read something and we like it, we don't care whether it took someone a long time or a short time to write it.

STRAND
I don't think the writer should care. We're lucky to write a few terrific things in our lifetime, and for all we know, we

may already have written them. So, who knows? I know nothing of the value of my work—all I know is that it's what I do, and what I love to do.

Strand at age thirty.

SHAWN

Did you feel differently when you were thirty? Because I did.

STRAND

Oh, I felt very differently. I was much more ambitious. I felt that I was destined to hold a special place. That's what I needed in those days to keep me writing. I don't need that any more, and I don't believe any of that obtains. But if young writers talk to me in those terms, I understand very well what they mean, and I'm sympathetic.

SHAWN

But all the same, doesn't it sometimes bother you that millions of people don't revere you? I mean, don't you sometimes feel that you ought to be honored for your accomplishments everywhere you go? After all, you *deserve* it.

STRAND

Well, some people like my poetry a great deal. It's better than *nobody* liking it.

SHAWN

But what about the millions of other people?

STRAND

There are a few people I know whose feeling about my poetry is the most important thing to me. It's as simple as that. I don't know many of the people who read my poems. I don't even know, when they read my poems, whether they like my poems. There's no way for me to know, so I can't worry about it. And if millions of people loved my poems, I'd wonder, In what way? What is it in my poems that appeals to so many people? I'd begin to wonder . . .

SHAWN

Yes, but all the same, don't you sometimes resent the fact that certain other people in our culture are so incredibly idolized? For example, I was recently listening to a CD of Elliott Carter, and I was thinking, Isn't it unbelievable that this man, who has created such incredibly subtle and beautiful music (including his settings of Elizabeth Bishop), is much less honored in our society than people who write songs using only three or four chords? Doesn't he have a reason to be outraged about that?

STRAND

Well, the people who like those three or four chords probably aren't going to like his music.

SHAWN

No.

STRAND

And he probably wouldn't want to be popular with that set.

SHAWN

No, he wouldn't.

STRAND

So there's no complaint.

SHAWN

You mean, these are two different audiences. So that would be like playing elephant music to giraffes.

STRAND

There is only one reason to be envious of those songwriters, and that is that they earn the kind of money that gives them a kind of freedom that Elliott Carter may not have. So it would be nice for Elliott Carter to go to the restaurants that Elton John can afford. But if the price is writing the kind of music that Elton John writes, he can do without it. And that's it. If I had to write the kind of sentences that Jacqueline Susann wrote, you know, write the kind of novels that she wrote, I wouldn't be able to hold my head high anywhere! I'd *slink* into restaurants—very expensive restaurants—and I'd *slink* into . . . expensive hotels. And I'd be ashamed to say what it was that I did.

SHAWN

But don't you find it sort of awful that our society doesn't even respect poetry enough to allow poets to support themselves through their writing?

STRAND

I think poetry would be different if people could make a living writing poetry. Then you would have to satisfy certain expectations. Instead of the inherited norms by which we recognize poems to be poems, there would be a whole new set of constraints, and not such enduring ones, having to do with the marketplace, having to do with what sells, or what engages people in the short run. So perhaps poetry is better off having no monetary value.

SHAWN

If I may speak of you personally, it seems that, for better or worse, writing poetry is an essential part of your identity, your sense of yourself—am I right about that?

STRAND

Well, my identity *is* hopelessly wrapped up in what I write, and my being a writer. If I stopped writing, I would simply feel the loss of myself. When I don't write, I don't feel properly alive. There was a period in my life, for five years, when I didn't write any poems. They were among the saddest years of my life, perhaps the saddest years. I wrote a lot of other things. None of them satisfied me the way the writing of poetry does, but I did them, just because I had to be ready, in case poetry came back into my life and I felt capable enough to write poems that weren't terrible. I refuse to write if I feel the poems I'm writing are bad. My identity is not that important, finally. Not dishonoring what I consider a noble craft is more important. I would rather not write than write badly and dishonor poetry—even if it meant I wasn't properly myself. I mean, this sounds high and noble, but in fact, it's not. I love poetry. I love myself, but I think I love poetry as much as I love myself.

SHAWN
You don't seem to share the attitude which some people have of, "Hey, I enjoy my hedonistic life of reading and writing, and I don't have the faintest idea whether what I do benefits society or not, and I couldn't care less."

STRAND
No. That's not my thing at all. I'm *certain* that what I do, and what other poets do, is important.

SHAWN
I have to ask you one more personal question. Well, I don't have to, but I will, because I'm curious: Do you care whether you're read after you're dead?

STRAND
Well, not to be funny about this, but I'm sort of split on the issue. I mean, I would like to be read after I'm dead, but that's projection.

SHAWN
You mean, because you're imagining . . . ?

STRAND
I mean, I'd really like to be *alive* after I'm dead. That's all that is. I don't really think it will make much difference to me when I'm dead whether I'm read or not.

SHAWN
Right.

STRAND
Just as whether I'm *dead* or not won't mean much to me when I'm dead. You see? Of course there are all those people who freeze themselves in those cryonic capsules. They just want to be and be and be. And sometimes I do too.

SHAWN

Sure. So the issue of whether your work is read after your death . . .

STRAND

I think most people who have published books, whose career is a matter of public record, will be read for a little while and then dropped. I mean, after a while, almost everybody is dropped to make room for the new. I think that's only fair. I just hope that the new, or the next, includes poetry. That's what I want. I think poetry is a fundamental human activity, and must continue. I think the minute we stop writing poetry, or reading it, we cease being human. Now, I can't be held to that, because there are very wonderful human beings who never read poetry, but I think it's one of the ways we understand ourselves, and know what it feels like to be alive, so that we don't turn into machines.

It's complicated, but I think it's this language, the language of poetry, through which we're recognizably human.

SHAWN

Or, to put the point a bit differently, it's this language, the language of poetry, that might make us feel glad that we *are* human, and somehow hopeful about the possibilities, rather than totally despairing. Well, anyway—you can get back to work.

Indelible Acts

A.L. Kennedy

It wasn't difficult.

"That's nice. That's nice."

Anyone could have done it—absolutely anyone.

"Just the way I like you. Great."

He'd been applying the usual friction, first and second fingertips. "Mm. Now the right," the circular rub and flicker insisting against cloth until both nipples caught at his attention, perked and ached. The way they would.

"Good." His lips slackened, were licked moist, while his interest hid in the dumb black of his glasses. "Very good." Laurie paused next, smiling, satisfied, happy my needs were symmetrically prominent. "Nice."

But anybody with hands could have done as much. Not even *hands*, necessarily: *hand* would have been enough; or a halfway decent prosthetic: even a properly placed domestic pet. Laurie wasn't working miracles—he was not involved with raising up the dead—only a little prickle or two of extremely erectile flesh. Brush or fluster them, breathe at them, kiss and they'll button up tight, they'll crest. Within their particular limits, the more you choose to find them, then the more there'll be to find—that's how they work, their inclinations are naturally salient. I can't do a thing to change them and neither can he—not fundamentally. A simple chill can prick them, as can that certain monthly tenderness, and then I'll be edged near precisely the same old slip of wet intentions he rubbed me to.

Traffic coughed and worried in the road beside us, pedestrians passed, among them a higher than average number of priests—or just men in cassocks, I'm not an expert, I can't say—and I wanted, very simply, to pummel Laurie onto his back and in some way secure him, then cut him out naked at the waist and suck him until both his balls were small as raisins, until he cried.

Because such impulses are irresistibly instinctive, they can't be helped. Primed past the point of caring, by no matter what or whom, I will react entirely predictably. Like the leopard with the zebra, like the lobster with the pot, I am part of Nature's usual arithmetic. I do often try to remember this in order to build perspective, an independently distant view.

Four nuns pattered by, soundless, their faces a little unlikely, surprised to be marooned in wimples. My breath barked against my sternum, abrasively needy, while social convention and mental discipline struggled to keep me from arrest. I said nothing, did nothing, only seethed, as might have been expected, queasy with lust.

Laurie grinned, knowingly unscathed. "You like it just as much as I do, don't you. Hm?"

"But not now." The day basted the avenue pleasantly: foreign monuments roiling under a classical sun and the Coliseum dark at Laurie's shoulder, a monstrous hoop of decay.

"Why not now?"

"Because people are looking, people will see."

"Then you shouldn't have worn that blouse—that's why

they're looking, so of course they'll see. Don't you like men staring at your tits? I do. Because they can't have you. Because you're mine."

Because you're mine. It's a standard wording, fits any mouth. I would have liked to turn it back on him, set *my* voice kicking in *his* chest, arcing that customary charge of hopefulness between the stomach and the throat. I would have liked to make it clear that: *because you're mine I will stand in the midst of clergy, stiff with the thought of your foreskin bitten back. Because you're mine I will be—with insufficient warning—simultaneously furious, beguiled, delighted, affronted, murderous and cheap. Because you're mine I will watch you the way that I'm watching right now and remember that I can strip you full down to the pink, the quick. I know you at least as well as you know me.*

Because you're mine. It's a standard wording, not dependent upon truth.

He's pacing now, almost trotting, round the walls, being interested about foundations and seating arrangements and herringbone brickwork, as displayed in flights of steps. He has an enthusiasm for constructions that I find I cannot share. But this is not a problem—I can sit here and write my letter while he prods about. And I can look at him moving through shudders of heat, the firmness of his shadow flexing, snug beneath him. He should wear a hat, really; by this evening he'll have burned. Laurie can be very cavalier about that kind of exposure.

I tend to be more careful because I have good skin. Most women of my age and younger have fine lines and visible wrinkles, but I don't. I have elasticity and bloom. I catch myself sometimes in the mirror when I'm alone and there it is—my beautiful outside—the ghosts of his hands still across it from the afternoons and evenings he's spent examining, testing flexibilities. I give him my best and he does appreciate it, he does take the time to say.

I also give him my collaboration, my consent, my long

bank-holiday weekend to pack up and use in a curtained and mirrored hotel room, in the moist, ecclesiastical heat of Rome. Since we flew in last night we've transgressed without dispensation, hourly, perhaps because no one who matters is here to see. I could, for example, cross to him now, take his hand, stroke the blue push of veins at his wrist and wriggle our palms together in an unmistakably familiar, casual, mutually affectionate and incriminating way that any malign observer could use against us. But this is a safe city; we have left Greenwich Mean Time and entered anonymity.

This makes Laurie happy, I can tell. His shoulders have a buoyancy about them I normally see only at night. In the dark he unfolds, relaxes, takes me outside, moves me up and down pavements we can't share with any kind of comfort in open day. Or else, he goes out driving, and I choose to come along, be where he takes me.

"Here?"

"Why not?" That time, we were in a field—lots of fresh air, healthy. "It's quiet, there's no one around." But his eyes still flickered across the windows, checking. Although he enjoys observing, Laurie never wants to be observed. He has a fear of being cornered or forced into actions he won't wish to take. "No interruptions, hm?"

I noted the bluey green of sheep's eyes, reflecting far off to the right. "It's raining."

"So you'll get wet."

He put on the hand brake and he turned the engine off and we sat in his car in the overcast dark of the field. No stars. On other nights, he might have picked the forest, or the underground office car park. I removed my mackintosh, kept on my shoes. High heels—impractical on grass.

"Oh, yes. Just what the doctor ordered. Let me see, though. Let me really see."

Because I wished to do so, needed to do so, had waited to do so, because this is a choice that I can make, I stepped out and crossed the turf to show him my skin. The bright burn of me flared in the headlamps, gleaming with drizzle and then moving, extinguishing under him.

"You're a very naughty, dirty girl."

Held safe between him and his car, I could feel his buttons against my spine, the thin chill of his zip, the tongue and groove of our mutual interest, of us being us together, our recoiling fit. I'd turned my head and could watch the blisters of rain on the bonnet shiver and split; a dim shining level with my eye.

He could have been anybody, "Lift your arse," but he was Laurie, working me tight with a smooth negation of all other possibilities.

I was glad of him, his cover, his cloth heat. My mother had often warned me against night air and stormy weather and being caught without a coat. Which made another reason to let Laurie catch me and—in a sense—lend me his.

"Good girl."

Anticipation faded into mud, the vague scent of animal shit and wet wool. He pressed my breath into fits and starts and came, as always, silently in a ragged burst of motion and then stillness, withdrawal. He's taught himself to be thoroughly secretive—which is why I've learned to read his body and his things. This afternoon I can tell he is contented, easy: he doesn't push at his hair too much, or tug his ears and there is something liquid in his stride, a muscular amusement, a tiny swing of appetite.

He's dressed to be comfy, but not unattractive. I saw him, warm and freshly woken, maybe seven hours ago, picking the right things and strolling between the wardrobe and the bed, naked in a way that made my gums hurt, made the palms of my hands start to twitch. I am designed to experience these feelings, they are hardwired through my whole anatomy. I consider types of insulation, circuit breaking, but every time he trips the switch and seems to prove I couldn't end this, that anything else would be inadequate.

Today, for example, he has equipped himself to show that he is happy and to jump-start my skull: white boxers (the pair I bought him) and his oldest jeans because we both know they hang well and make it look more than likely that he does, too. Add in the plain black T-shirt to set off the linen jacket for thumb-hooking over his shoulder and the Ray-Bans for making sure that he won't need to squint and there he is, my Laurie, all tooled up.

Back at home he'll leave clothes with me: accessories, bits and bobs: small records of his scent and shape. Leather is most eloquent; his belts roll where they've taken the curve of his back and notch to mark the measure of his waist, his shoes and gloves reform against his movements and his sweat. And, of course, I do the same. In his absence, the pattern of his previous needs sings out on me. He's oiled into the grain of my fingers the way any habit would be. It is unsurprising that, at night, I can find his memory shunts me into sleeplessness.

I haven't tried to sleep in Rome, not yet. It has seemed unnecessary. Fatigue occasionally dives at me, unsteadies reality, but I won't give in. I'm going to stay more than conscious, because Laurie is all here with me: leaned over the railing, nicely taut and shifting: my encyclopedia. Before we leave, before it's over, I'll know his arms by heart, from the short clip of his fingernails to the paler and paler tenderness of his joints, the soft rise of hair. Anyone can concentrate, stay alert, for only four days and three nights when they're constantly accompanied by the body they've learned to miss. I am always greedy for what I know I'll lack.

Of course, this rationing and waiting will tend to breed intensity in us both.

"Tell me where to aim it."

The accumulated discomfort of over-rehearsed desire.

"Or I'll just put it where I want."

In Rome, I'm moving from the grease of his imagination to his everyday coughs and whispers, his small breaths when he's reading and the way he towels his hair. Each part of this is as addictive as I'd guessed, as hard to walk away from, or to fight.

"I'll put it where I want it. And you know where I'll want..."

I'm more used to the short nights when we're trying to

impress. They were when I pushed for something to stay with me while he did not, for marks, for brands in the memory, indelible acts. I have, in the past, been anxious to experiment with error and trial: squatting, or standing, or bending or lying in my bath.

"*That's* where I'll want. Right there. And there."

"Laurie . . ." The not unpleasant smell of it, almost herbal, slightly bitter, grassy, hot. "Laurie, could you—"

"What?"

"Well. It isn't . . . erotic."

He was standing unfastened, braced. "I'm *pissing on you*, how can that not be erotic?" He rubbed through his fringe with his free hand.

"It's mainly just warm—more relaxing than anything. I'm sorry."

"It's not erotic." His flow relented, sputtered, stopped. "Not at all?"

"I'm sorry."

He sat on the edge of the bath with his back to me, set his hands on his knees to lean forward and away. "No, don't be sorry."

"It was good to try."

"Yeah." He looked at his watch. "I don't really have time now for anything else."

I hate Laurie's watch. Resistant to many varieties of highly unnatural shock and proofed against pressures and waters at hideous depths, it will most certainly outlive us. It pecks out our time together unremittingly, it's his conscience and my limit and I wish he'd agreed just to leave it in our room. I don't want to be reminded of when we'll stop. I don't want to be sad yet and have to tell him why.

I want to keep collecting and making his inventory complete without distractions. When I go home, he'll have soaked my recollection, my blood will smell of him, I will think with his voice and be able to be alone, to be with *other* people and to comfortably keep in mind all I'll need of him.

I do hope that, eventually, this could be true: that Laurie could come to be anyone, the next one, someone new.

He's craning over. He shouldn't do that, it leaves the skin between his hair and his collar bared to the sun. He's tender there, sweet to kiss, and this is not what he *does*: something repeatable, replaceable, easy to find again. This is what he *is*. This is the unrepeatable, irreplaceable, unforgivable man I have had to do without for years, holding on, numb between installments of whatever his household arrangements allow him to give. This is the best he can bring me: it's what should have stopped us becoming ridiculous. This should have prevented the evenings full of ice cubes and safety razors and fruit and all the other variations on our theme—a little bite of toothpaste, a little KY dip, escalating restraint.

"Dirty girl."

"No, you're the one that's dirty. Dirty old man."

He only grinned, untying me, showing he'd taken no offense. "No, *you're* the one and you're going to prove it. Go and get that thing—I want to see. Show me how you're a bad girl—playing while I'm away . . ."

"The people at work bought it for me."

"But you use it."

"Yes, I do."

I fetched it through for him, still in the box, so that he could unveil it.

"Fuck."

My implement was longer, fatter—unmistakably larger than his. Which should have been of no significance to him. At least a couple of inches were just there for grip, they weren't a requirement, they didn't establish a level of need. He turned it in his hands like a condensed adultery.

"Fuck."

But I don't think he ever considered not using it.

"All right, then. All right." The dark of his eye coolly mirroring my skin. "You always want things to remember . . . Well, all right."

And I do remember, absolutely clearly, the moment when the pain of his being there exceeded the pain of his having to leave me be.

Laurie and I, we don't discuss that night, it's a secret we keep from each other. We don't tell. I find, more and more, that I write out what happened in letters I never post—letters to a wife I do not know. We must have a few things in common, though, that's what I'd suppose. We must both look at him, walking in sunlight, and find him beautiful.

L'histoire du soldat
Kurt Vonnegut

A production of this work with a new text was envisioned by Robert Johnson, the artistic director of the New York Philomusica Chamber Ensemble. Feeling that the rather tepid Charles-Ferdinand Ramuz fairy tale hardly suited the times (World War I) or caught the character of a soldier deserting the killing grounds of the Western Front, he thought instantly that Kurt Vonnegut, himself a prisoner of war in World War II and a survivor of the bombing of Dresden (Slaughterhouse Five) would be a perfect choice to provide a completely new accompaniment to Stravinsky's music. In January, 1993, Vonnegut completed the text, changing the venue to World War II and picking Pvt. Eddie Slovik, the first US soldier executed for desertion since the Civil War, for his lead character. There have been a number of productions of the work, the first in Alice Tully Hall, May 6, 1993, starring Eli Wallach, Ann Reinking, Malcolm Gets, and Martin Vidnovic, choreographed and directed by Patricia Birch.

CAST: Major General, Soldier, Military Police Sergeant, Red Cross Girl, Two Ordinary Infantry Privates

L'HISTOIRE DU SOLDAT

PROLOGUE

GENERAL: Good evening. *L'histoire du soldat*, in English *A Soldier's Story*, has until now been performed as it was premiered in 1918, in peaceful Switzerland when World War I, in which eight million soldiers died, was going on. Bursts of brilliant music by the great Igor Stravinsky alternate with spoken words written by the composer's Swiss friend, the novelist Charles-Ferdinand Ramuz. Neither collaborator had ever been a soldier. The story Ramuz wrote to go with Stravinsky's music is based on an intentionally silly, whimsical Russian folktale, supposedly about a soldier. But this soldier is unlike any real soldier in all of history. How is he armed? With a rifle? With grenades? With a spear? With a violin, friends and neighbors. A violin! That's it! Let's hope it doesn't rain.

He is all alone, as a real soldier almost never is—a private without comrades, without a superior to tell him what to do next. Does he run into an enemy? Or at least into a military policeman, who asks him what in hell he's doing away from his unit, and armed with nothing but a violin? Not this soldier. He runs into a devil, who offers him great riches and the favors of a beautiful noblewoman, in exchange for violin lessons. To protest that this soldier isn't a real soldier would be like protesting that the wolf in Prokofiev's *Peter and the Wolf* isn't a real wolf—in yet another lighthearted Russian folktale set to music. (*Pause.*) To protest that the soldier isn't a real soldier would be perfectly inane, if it weren't for this: Igor Stravinsky's music, possibly in unconscious response to the sufferings and deaths of millions of real soldiers not far away, is anything but innocent. Its folkloric merriment is so soured by wry melodic ironies that it might in fact be a setting for a real down-and-dirty soldier's story.

We propose to prove this—as I become the commander of an American infantry division invading Germany very near the end of World War II. Our front is three miles (*pointing left*) in that direction. It is under heavy bombardment—an erupting earth under an exploding sky and a blizzard of razor blades. Not nice.

PART I—THE SOLDIER'S MARCH

GENERAL: (*Wry, weary, humane*)
A victory march?
Almost. Not quite,
The enemy capital
Is nearly in sight.
The decisive battles
Have all been fought and won.
In a very short time, now,
This war will be done.
So I order my men,
Children, actually, and far from home,
To fight and die for nothing.
(SOLDIER *enters left, goofy, dazed.*)
What the hell are you supposed to be?
No rifle, no helmet, no pack.
What a sad, sad sack!

SOLDIER: A sack of shit. I quit. I quit.

GENERAL: Snap to attention! Salute! Salute!

SOLDIER: That's all over for me.
You can have my fucking soldier suit.
(*Shell-shocked, singing dreamily*)
We don't want no more of your bullshit,
We don't want no more of your bullshit.
We don't want no more of your bullshit.
We just want to go home.

GENERAL: Where are you supposed to be today?

SOLDIER: Where all the people are getting killed.
So I ran away.

GENERAL: That's all you've got to say?

SOLDIER: If you knew me, you'd know
That all my life I've run away.
Never asked to be born in the first place.

GENERAL: You couldn't have run away to a worse place.

L'HISTOIRE DU SOLDAT

	I can have you shot for being here.
SOLDIER:	All I want is what we're fighting for.
GENERAL:	Which is?
SOLDIER:	Freedom from fear.
	(SOLDIER *laughs helplessly*.)
	Kyuk kyuk kyuk.

PART II—AIRS BY A STREAM

GENERAL:	(*Calling*) MP! MP!
	(MP *enters smartly, salutes*.)
MP:	Sir!
GENERAL:	Take this disgusting wreck somewhere
	And wring his neck.
MP:	Company G, or I miss my guess.
	Artillery had their range.
	One hell of a mess.
	Probably one of the replacements
	Came in last night.
	(*To* SOLDIER) That right?
SOLDIER:	(*Airily*) Howdy do.
GENERAL:	A pitiful sight!
	The human trash they send us now,
	And they're supposed to fight!
	Arrest this creep,
	And charge him with desertion
	In the face of the enemy.
	(*To* SOLDIER)
	You are about to become infamous
	All the way to Supreme Headquarters.
SOLDIER:	Little old me?
	Just a P.V.T.?
GENERAL:	You'll see.
SOLDIER:	The guy in the foxhole with me,
	He quit, too.
GENERAL:	(*Emptily*) Whoop-dee-doo.
	What was his name?
SOLDIER:	Should have been Fountain.

GENERAL: Fountain? (*To* MP) Write that down.
MP: Yes, sir!
SOLDIER: That's what his neck was
After his head fell off.

PART III—THE SOLDIER'S MARCH
(SOLDIER *and* MP *in ruined farmhouse*)
SOLDIER: Nice place we have here. I'm a very lucky louse.
MP: Used to be a farmer's house.
This is where an enemy sniper died.
They blew off the roof,
And shot out the windows
With him inside.
SOLDIER: Died a hero. What a way to go.
Somebody should tell his mother so.
MP: His helmet hangs over there
On a rusty nail,
And this former family dwelling
Is now a makeshift jail.
SOLDIER: Cozy.
MP: It is now my duty, captured coward,
Who could take no more,
To read aloud to you
Article Number Fifty-eight
From the Articles of War.
SOLDIER: My mother used to read aloud to me
Before I went sleepy-bye.
MP: Article Number Fifty-eight is about (*pause*)
Going sleepy-bye.
SOLDIER: Love it already!
MP: (*Reading*) "The penalty for misbehavior
In the face of the enemy—"
SOLDIER: Never saw one.
MP: "Shall be dishonorable discharge
From the service—"
SOLDIER: (*Gaily*) Can I go home now?
MP: "Forfeiture of all pay and allowances—"

SOLDIER: (*Mockingly*) Boo-hoo.
MP: "And being shot to death
By a firing squad."
SOLDIER: I'm dead. I'm dead.
MP: Didn't you hear what I said?
They haven't shot anybody in this man's army
For what you did since 1865,
Since the Civil War!
Not one American was shot for cowardice
During the Spanish-American War.
Not one American was shot for cowardice
During the First World War.
And nobody is going to be shot for cowardice
In this damn war.
You're as safe as you'd be in your mother's arms.
SOLDIER: You don't know my mother, brother.
Or my bad luck.
MP: (*Impatiently*) Oh fuck!
A couple of years in prison,
Ten years at most.
You'll be well-fed,
And warm as toast.

PART IV—PASTORALE
(RED CROSS GIRL *enters, stops at imaginary doorway.*)
RED CROSS: (*Aside*) The Red Cross girl.
I'm their mother, their sister,
The girl next door—
When what they need, so close to
Death, is a brainless whore,
A hole—
A piece of meat with leaky orifices,
Which is what they've become,
Diddley dum, diddley dum.
(*Calling*) Anybody in there?
Red Cross. Red Cross.
MP: (*To* SOLDIER) Who says you're not lucky?

	Red Cross!
	She can get you coffee and doughnuts,
	Shaving cream, toothpaste and dental floss.
	If you were an officer,
	She might fuck you.
	Since you are an enlisted man,
	She will duck you,
	And your cow-eyed pleas for relief.
RED CROSS:	(*Aside*) Good grief!
	As though I weren't an angel of mercy,
	But a rank-happy sex-appeal abuser.
SOLDIER:	Don't tell her I'm a loser. Don't tell her what I did, that I ran away.
MP:	Entrez, mademoiselle, s'il vous plait.
	(*Aside*) Feminine sex appeal corrupts.
	Feminine sex appeal near the front corrupts Absolutely.
	That she sleeps with the general
	Is common knowledge.
RED CROSS:	(*Aside*) Not because he's a general,
	But because we've both been to college.
	He went to West Point,
	I went to Bryn Mawr.
MP:	(*Aside*) Har de har har.
RED CROSS:	I'm here to pay your prisoner a call.
MP:	No prisoner in here at all, at all.
	Just me and my heroic buddy here.
SOLDIER:	(*Aside*) Nobody here but us chickens.
RED CROSS:	Oh dear. I wonder where they've got him.
MP:	Search me.
SOLDIER:	Search me.
RED CROSS:	You think they've already shot him?
MP:	They don't shoot deserters anymore.
	(*To* SOLDIER) Tell her.
SOLDIER:	They don't shoot deserters anymore.
RED CROSS:	You haven't heard? Here's the latest word:
	Supreme Headquarters has just made a decision

L'HISTOIRE DU SOLDAT

                Which sickens the commander of this division.
                The deserter he's put under arrest
                Is to be made a lesson for all the rest.
                And killed.
SOLDIER: (*A two-note song*) Bing-go.

PART V—AIRS BY A STREAM

                (*Same farmhouse.* SOLDIER *sitting, inert, resigned,* MP *standing.* GENERAL *enters.* MP *snaps to attention, salutes.*)
MP: (*Barking*) A-ten-hut!
                (SOLDIER *stays seated.* GENERAL *stands over him.*)
GENERAL: On your feet!
                SOLDIER: (*Inert, expecting to be taken to execution*)
                I'm ready. Make it short and sweet.
GENERAL: You're not going to be shot.
                You're going back to your platoon.
SOLDIER: Take a flying fuck at the moon.
                I'd just run away again,
                If I wasn't killed before I could do it.
                So screw it.
GENERAL: In violation of orders
                From Supreme Headquarters,
                I've offered you a chance to go on living,
                And you just blew it.
SOLDIER: I'm no damn good.
                Never was.
                So get it over with.
MP: What about your folks?
SOLDIER: Sorry they ever had me.
                Look at me!
                Me and my
                Folks are dirty jokes.
GENERAL: A girl? A wife?
SOLDIER: No girl, no wife, no fucking life.
                Get it over with!

GENERAL: (GENERAL *does dementia dance*.)
Act like a raving maniac!
Put on a really zany act.
Be so sick and crazy that you never should have
Passed your draft physical in the first place.
And save your butt!
SOLDIER: I'm not a nut.
I'm just a disgrace
To the human race.
At least it won't hurt much.
At least I'll know who did it and why,
Which is more than I'd know
If I were some poor runt at the front.
At least it won't leave me a cripple.
Get it over with!

PART VI—THE SOLDIER'S MARCH

(GENERAL *and* RED CROSS *in his office. He is seated, she stands behind him, massaging his neck and shoulders.*)
GENERAL: "For this relief much thanks;
'Tis bitter cold,
And I am sick at heart."
RED CROSS: A general quoting William Shakespeare!
GENERAL: The world is full of surprises, dear.
West Point was my joint,
But my father was an English teacher.
RED CROSS: Mine was a preacher.
GENERAL: After years of faithful and honorable service
To my nation,
I am now under orders to commit
What either of our fathers
Would declare an abomination.
For me, Betty,
And for my beloved division,
It will be
An utterly undeserved humiliation.

	(RED CROSS *stops massage, moves away, spooked*.)
RED CROSS:	Betty is dead. My name is Caroline.
GENERAL:	What happened to Betty?
RED CROSS:	She had body lice.
GENERAL:	We all do. (*He scratches himself.*)
RED CROSS:	On her way to the delousing station, Betty stepped on a mine. (*Scratches herself.*) The lice lived through it.
GENERAL:	If anybody can, the lice can do it. (*Pause, with* RED CROSS *considering him and their empty relationship from a distance.*)
RED CROSS:	You must have sent many boys to die.
GENERAL:	Without batting an eye— In North Africa, and Sicily and France. But every one of them had a fighting chance. I now find myself the only American officer In eighty years to be ordered To stage a shameful dance, With some poor, weak son of a bitch Who has probably shit in his pants, And shoot him. Some show! It'll let every soldier know That he can be killed for entertainment.
RED CROSS:	Entertainment for who?
GENERAL:	Somebody at Supreme H.Q. (*He scratches himself.*) Son of a bitch! Oh, how I itch!

PART VII—THE ROYAL MARCH

(GENERAL, RED CROSS, SOLDIER *and* MP *do lice dance, scratching. All but* SOLDIER *and* MP *exit, setting next scene, which is back in farmhouse.* SOLDIER *is seated, happily writing with pencil on a pad.*)

MP:	You've already made quite an impression On people who would really Rather not shoot you. What more do you hope to accomplish With a written confession?
SOLDIER:	I want everybody to know it's okay, What they have to do. The more I think about it, The less reason there is to raise A stink about it. I always wanted to do something good. Nobody ever thought I could. All of a sudden, guess what? I can give my life for my country. Other soldiers will fight better because of me.
MP:	(*Vomiting sounds*) Bluhh. Uhhh. (*etc.*) (RED CROSS *enters, carrying a paperback booklet, an army manual, stops at imaginary door.*)
RED CROSS:	Red Cross! Red Cross!
MP:	(*To* SOLDIER *ironically*) Coffee and doughnuts, shaving cream, Toothpaste and dental floss. (*To* RED CROSS): Entrez, mademoiselle, s'il vous plait.
RED CROSS:	(*Entering*) How is the prisoner this awful day?
SOLDIER:	(*Cheerfully*) I'm all set to play.
MP:	He says it's all okay.
RED CROSS:	The general will do anything to stop it, If only you'll cooperate.
SOLDIER:	(*Radiant*) I'm giving the orders now.
RED CROSS:	You've turned the general, Who's one in a million, Into a chickenhearted civilian.
SOLDIER:	(*Radiant*) Tough shit for him.
RED CROSS:	He sent this book. He thought you ought to have a look.

L'HISTOIRE DU SOLDAT

MP: It's an army manual written in 1863.
The Civil War.
SOLDIER: It's just for me?
RED CROSS: (*Hauntedly*) We'll see. We'll see.
It's still in print. This copy's mint.
(SOLDIER *takes manual.*)
You now have in your hands,
Along with your own life,
So help you God,
The official manual
For the organization and duties
Of a firing squad.
SOLDIER: Somebody must be really pissed off at me.
Who could it be?
So mightily pissed off
At little me.

PART VIII—THE LITTLE CONCERT

MP: (*Reading*)
"The place of execution will be prepared to provide
For a back wall made of absorbent material, before
Which the prisoner will be placed.
An upright post
Will be placed in front of the back wall,
And will be used to support the prisoner
If necessary.
If, while the condemned is being prepared for,
Or marched to,
The place of execution,
Collapse has taken place
Or is imminent,
A suitable braceboard
And straps
Will be adjusted."

PART IX—THREE DANCES

   (GENERAL *tangos with* RED CROSS, SOLDIER *with* MP.
   GENERAL *exits, leaving* SOLDIER, RED CROSS *and* MP
   to continue previous scene.)
SOLDIER: (*Reading aloud, with* MP *raising his hand whenever
   sergeant is mentioned*)
   "A firing squad in charge of a sergeant,
   Consisting of not less than eight
   And no more than twelve enlisted men"—
   (*Aside*) All pals of mine—
   "Enlisted men skilled in the use
   Of the regulation rifle"—
   (*Aside*) I used to have one of those.
   Easy come, easy go—
   "Will be selected by the officer designated
   To carry out the act
   Of execution.
   When the hood has been adjusted,
   And the signal given that the prisoner
   Is in final readiness,
   The firing squad
   Will be marched by the sergeant
   To a designated spot
   And formed in a single or double rank,
   Facing the prisoner,
   And not less than twenty paces from him.
   The members of the firing squad
   Will be armed with regulation rifles,
   Each of which will have been loaded
   And the pieces locked by the officer
   Charged with the execution of the sentence.
   One of the rifles will contain a blank round,
   And the identity of this piece will not
   Be disclosed."

PART X—THE DEVIL'S DANCE

   (GENERAL *enters left and* RED CROSS *retreats to right,
   to serve as observers, while* MP *and* SOLDIER *and two*

L'HISTOIRE DU SOLDAT

other ENLISTED MEN *dance a pantomime of taking* SOLDIER *from place of confinement to place of execution, tying to a post, and putting a hood over his head.*)

GENERAL: So we shot him.

PART XI—LITTLE CHORALE

GENERAL: His last words were—
SOLDIER: (SOLDIER *removes hood, takes time before speaking.*)
They'd better be good.
(*Experimenting unseriously*)
How much wood could a woodchuck chuck,
If a woodchuck could chuck wood?
GENERAL: His last words were—
SOLDIER: (*Experimenting*)
Oh, beautiful for spacious skies,
For amber waves of grain.
GENERAL: His last words were—
SOLDIER: With my life all through,
These words will have to do:
(*Pause*)
Remember me.
(*Silence.* ALL *onstage are drained, sick of the story, no longer military, becoming actors in the present, having done a job they didn't like.* GENERAL *strips off tunic.* MP *and two* ENLISTED MEN *get rid of helmet liners, throw them away or whatever.* SOLDIER *remains at the stake, still a troubling figure.*)
GENERAL: (*To audience, a casual host once more*)
No more acting.
(*To* SOLDIER) Not coming down from the cross?
SOLDIER: In a minute.
GENERAL: No rush.
SOLDIER: (*Sepulchrally*)
There's something else the people here should know.

GENERAL:	Indeed. Would you like to tell?
SOLDIER:	Let a woman tell.
RED CROSS:	By process of elimination that must be me. *(Pulls herself together, takes center stage)* Okay. This new libretto is based very loosely on the true story of the execution of an American private, a friendless replacement sent at once to a unit under heavy artillery fire. It was too much for him. He was terrified. He ran away. His name was Eddie D. Slovik.
MP:	Serial number 36896415. The first number, three, indicates that he hadn't volunteered. Eddie Slovik was a draftee, a poor boy from a Polish neighborhood in Detroit, who had been arrested once for petty thievery.
SOLDIER:	Eddie Slovik confessed that he had deserted. He said he would do it again, if he was forced to fight.
RED CROSS:	*(Pleading his case)* That's how Eddie Slovik was. Under fire, Eddie became what he was born to be.
SOLDIER:	A deserter from G Company, 109th Infantry.
GENERAL:	Twenty-eighth Infantry Division, which was engaged in heavy fighting near the French village of Elbeuf.
ALL:	Poor son of a bitch!
GENERAL:	All this can be found in a splendid book by William Bradford Huie, *The Execution of Private Slovik*.
SOLDIER:	Now out of print.
GENERAL:	Published in 1954.

PART XII—DEVIL'S SONG

SOLDIER:	Eddie Slovik, the only American soldier Executed for cowardice Since the Civil War,

L'HISTOIRE DU SOLDAT

	And to the present day. He died of multiple bullet wounds At 10:04 in the morning, On January 31, 1945.
GENERAL:	Instantly! That much we know.
SOLDIER:	Easy come. Easy go. Private Slovik had no last words. We put those words in his mouth:
ALL:	Remember me.
RED CROSS:	He was shot in a French garden in the wintertime.

PART XIII—GREAT CHORALE

RED CROSS:	I showed our libretto to a Russian émigré, and he couldn't believe it.
GENERAL:	Couldn't believe what?
RED CROSS:	Thousands of soldiers were shot by their own armies in two world wars for running away from the enemy: Russians, Germans, Italians, British, French. You name it. It made no sense to him to hear That we, the United States of America, Had executed Exactly one. He thought we must be crazy.
SOLDIER:	The man who signed Eddie Slovik's death warrant was General of the Armies Dwight David Eisenhower.
ALL:	Ike.
GENERAL:	Years later, General Eisenhower, then retired from the presidency to his estate in Gettysburg, Pennsylvania, was asked by the historian Bruce Catton to comment on the unique position in American military history to which he had assigned Eddie Slovik. And the general is said by Catton to have Replied—

MP:	May I?
GENERAL:	By all means.
MP:	(*Impersonating Eisenhower*)
	As a matter of fact, I approved that one.
	It was for a repeated case of desertion.
	The man refused to believe
	That he would ever be executed.
	At the very last moment,
	I sent my judge advocate general to see him.
	And I said,
	"If you will go back and serve in your
	company honorably, and until this war is over,
	you'll get an honorable discharge, and not the
	death sentence."
	He said, "Baloney," or words to that effect.
ALL:	(*Continuing impersonation*)
	And so he was executed.

THE TRIUMPHAL MARCH OF THE DEVIL

THE END

Rachel Hadas

Searching the Scriptures

Sunny May morning; going through the mail.
Among solicitations, one stands out
from summer neighbors: a Conquer-a-thon—
so many laps jogged; dollars pledged per lap.
The logo on the Union Christian Baptist
School's envelope: a bearded helmeted
head; a scroll reading CONQUERORS; below it
in smaller letters Rom. 8:37.
To check the reference is a moment's work.
Here's the Epistle. *Nay*, Paul writes the Romans,
*in all these things we are more than conquerors
through him that loved us.*

I sit, the Bible open on my lap.
And as I move to shut the book again,
a small pink piece of paper flutters out
from earlier in the New Testament:
an office memo, blank. But on its back
in red ink capitals in a clear hand:
Luke 12:49–53.

Clearly it is premature to close
this mystic tome without a second time
checking a reference. I turn to Luke,
not without some sense of what I'll find.
Sure enough, the passage is in red.
Divinity is talking; listen up!
Vermillion words rise from the page like smoke:
I am come to send fire to earth.

And what will I, if it be already kindled?
Then (testily, it seems to me) *Suppose ye*
I am come to give peace on earth? I tell you Nay,
but rather division. The father
shall be divided against the son
and the son against the father.

As is well known, the book is so constructed
scenarios concocted come undone,
reshuffle, recombine, float free again.
Fragments of plot, divided families
sparkle on the surface of a sea
boiling bloody myriads have drowned in.
Or does that sea politely part to let
a virtuous remnant pass? This piece of paper
torn from *medias res* of a short life,
some family drama or some faded rage,
is what I'm holding in my hand this minute.
I turn the blushing faces of the code
back toward each other, shut the book,
and shelve it with its secret still intact.
Its many secrets.
                      Union Christian Baptist
Conquer-a-thon. $1.50 might
possibly be sufficient per lap;
the child who will be running just turned ten.

Three Poems by Richard Lamb

Margaret Trudeau's "Pied Beauty"

That night I met Jorge, a Peruvian racing driver . . .
                              Margaret Trudeau

CANADIAN POLITICS

There is finitude in ice and icy finitude
in public realms. The *of-a-pieceness* of it. It
maddened me, I wanted life to shatter. Glitter
like jewely fragments so I might admire. Rude
governance was not for me: I loved rage.
                    Its edges caught the light.

THE PM's CHATELAINE

I yearned for yielding to purely private power;
hostess to pols, hockey oafs, the Queen's retinue.
(My skirt too short for that occasion scolded
the press.) The result: *Margaret disparue*.
              I had affairs, you had affairs
of state. Who was cuckolded?

VACANCE

We met, I saw you stern, your cool opacity
seemed weighty—the ballast that I craved.
You loved my flighty dance, my warm vivacity.
That moment in Tahiti, who was saved?
And who—brakes' screech, the music
of broken glass—encountered tragedy?

STUDIO 54

Desire loomed irregular, all was mine:
privacy, glamour. It was in the magazines.
A girl needs some attention for herself. That it
come from Mick or Jack—so much the better.
And drugs were fun, but then the drug was Thorazine.
      Don't think I was so blithe.

Roman Polanski's "Annabel Lee"

KRAKÓW

Childe Roman, war-stricken.
Witness to massed hobnails, tanks' rumble.
      Mother, pregnant, taken.
Nocturnal jaunts for crusts, rinds, gristle.

In the end survival. Film school, then fade
from gray montage. (Death. Ancientness
      and ancient persecutions.)
To the Summer of Love and ensuing Me Decade.

LA-LA LAND

Chrome hurtles from an asphalt cloverleaf.
Irrigated sprawl, ochre tones of thirsty earth.
There's Robert Evans in a James Bond suit!
              Unkempt suburban youth.

Some turning-on and tuning-out. The cant
and serendipities of tripster shills.
      None of this was me.
I believed in effort. The rich twist of wills.

ON HORROR

I tried to tell you about it using
your own streets and houses.
How it seeps, invades the mundane
so that those two things keep fusing.

My own world's really as elegant
and utilitarian as a carcass.
Sade and Masoch provide its fission.
               Dynamos of imposition.

HORROR

She unruffled, stunning, young, unscathed.
        Then scathed—and but a child.
Our connection? The dark similitude
between an unbuilt city and a city razed.

My appeal: Foreignness. Intricacy.
       Success, I suppose, impressed her.
A childish veneer. (Did she ever conceive—
       that I was a child molester?)

Bernie Cornfeld's "Ozymandias"

INVESTORS OVERSEAS SERVICES

There I was, rumpled, pudgy, balding, all of five
foot six, ex-Brooklyn College, the Merchant Marine
—Look what we did! my fund of mutual funds
         once had two billion under management.

My plan was "people's capitalism": Get Rich!
    I said. I certainly did. Those
I'd gathered round me did too. Losers and drifters.
Lone wolves often yearn to be joiners.

LAISSEZ-FAIRE

It was a little like one of those movie star
fan clubs. Join up, we'll issue you an ID card
and company attaché—suddenly you're
                The Sort of Man Who Reads *Playboy*!

So think, when you hear that familiar
French phrase, of holy writ:
the incantatory *let*: Let there be light.
Let there be income! Let come what may.

ON SALESMANSHIP

You have to take control to sell. You tell people
where to sit. Ask for water, a cup of coffee.
       They'll warm to you that way.
But just as we have a subdivided nervous

system (antagonistic parts of which control
       erection, ejaculation), so
a shift from sell to let them buy has to occur.
Let it happen. Just stay calm and you'll close the deal.

THE LONE AND LEVEL SANDS

By '68 my head, my sneer of cold command
adorned newsweeklies. I drove a Maserati
(orange in hue), owned a French chateau.
My name was linked with starlets.

Of course some regulatory agency
always objects to detritus—the scattered
shells of dummy corporations—to Gordian
knots cut and Sabine retirees, their savings gone . . .

ON DIETING

Okay, I cut some corners.
I have an Alexandrine approach to life. Cut

the knot. Like losing weight: eat all you want.
                    That's my philosophy.

(I'm partial to pastrami. Have it flown in.)
        Then—can you think of anything
simpler?—you just vomit. I mean people tend
to make things so *complicated* for themselves . . .

Three Poems by Neil Azevedo

Camille sur son Lit de Mort

Claude, be still, light
is what you're seeing now:
the moon contained in dusk,
the dark meadow a mist.
My shadows are the shape of flowers.
But the parlor fills with gray,
and sparrows, failing to reach
inside, are the fingers of the sun.

Is it snowing? I am silence gathered
from glass, quiet as reflection,
useless sun on water. Think of my heart
as Cézanne's trees: black—suddenly still,
and my skin as forever in breeze.
How does it feel? Touch the window,
now my hand.

No daylight ghosts among my flesh.
I am a candle pulling at the dark.
I am a *torchère*, my incandescent bowl
swallowing the room, whole,
one thing that is what all eyes seek.
Am I pleasing
in my dress? Claude, I do

not want to be bad light:
a moth dying, its friable wings,
or, filtered through the wings,
operatic light. Let me always,
at thirty-two, almost empty
into darkness, finally,
until that's what I become:

the sound of a bible,
Les Glaçons, Les Rochers à Belle-Îsle,
light trapped in morning mist
around *L' Eglise à Vernon*.
Soon the sun will return
like a citizen. But in the dark,
a black leaf, I speak.

Discarded Nude

I know now where I am
and am afraid. This dark
behind me found me trying

for light from the window.
Could you enter, once again,
what's possible, what you made?

Twenty summers since my face
(am I slightly unattractive
—I mean my wizened nose,

I mean my fading cheek) . . .
I am almost beautiful, too.
Step up to my pale neck.

Is *Still Life with Fruit* done?
Or did you also adumbrate
that dark grape, that silent bowl?

Come whisper. Slip your touch
across my mess of browns;
wet your fingers, stroke me

with a blush of wine.
Let brushes, soft as lashes,
lift stillness from my flesh:

My hands? Fuck *The Sower*—
his arm cocked into the sun.
At least create my hands.

Where you touched me last,
canvas's gaunt shade. Dry—
a desert I can remember

as I can remember floods
of color—each rosy scumble
working out my limbs.

See this unshaped thigh?
Your fingers were a wind
when you came close,

hands busy on my skin
industrious across my . . .
This is how I always begin:

no sun, though you make suns,
no child, no world of cyclamen.
I never had a name.

Will White #4
be your pressure on my throat,
my body whisper-still?

I know now where I am.

Caspar Hauser Songs

*St. Joseph's Center for Mental Health,
Adolescent Ward, 1989*

1. The Dark Lament of His Mouth

Before I was done being born, earthlight
cluttered the floor: small insects fingered my back
and chest, my walls tranquil with the velvet
drape of roots and with cement's cold breath.
In a chain's motion, I heard the mole's thoughts
in darkness lit by my hands, I heard my heart
and the writhing tails of rats. I broke
(as an act of silence) their awful paws,
felt my way into a voice I held
inside my claws as birds resemble sleep.
That was where I saw my Other—the body
I could please, a fog on the dark glass
nocturnal in reflection, my veiled vessel
to whom I said, *I want to be a horseman.*

2. Solitude

And now, a child, there on the floor, quiet
as wood; when smiling, a ceramic bowl,
and ceasing to be or finding myself
still—light dimming my invisible veins.
Always on Advent eve, the horror glass,
sterility of the clock, fingers thrilled
with a fire, the whole world in bed early.
Strange illuminations. From my room,
earth's darkness miles deep. And so it begins
in the auspices of rain, in getting up
from the glass, loosening water, in men,
in their laughter, in memorizing tricks.
This is the silent genius of the deaf—
eyes watering, lips wondering: "Jesus."

3. Whiteness

Closer to gods I enter my limp, carefully
step through heaven, where children sully
hot stone, where we keep to ourselves,
most things the burnished pearl of owl's
claw, *snow in siege*, the eyes of community
painless light. Where boys become a human room
for animals to fight; slim breeds,
thin as the thief's hand, as the plum's skin,
bleed. Where those that come closest die.
Then pleasure. Then we speak the language
restive from a throat, wild, an ugly
tongue by which I will consider these
new things (away from the room) you—like my
rat-bloodied hand, like my sacred heart.

4. On the Albino Farm

The artisans assume their human shape.
Their practiced claws wake to find my name,
to carve me into fruit, my likeness veiled
beneath the harvest of the field. In heat
the sheets haunt stalks; in their drained skin
they discover winter, scurry for a snow
they plant deep into the color of men.
The specters hear me speak, they listen
for my voice and feed. The demons live
inside my speech and stutter in my throat—
they make me say the things I didn't mean
and search the earth for sound. They sing without
a voice. They wait to live, dissolve to sleep.
They eat. They burn. They harbor all the deaf.

5. First Light

Smoke travels from a burning horse
injured by the dark, then slaughtered.
Flames finger its shape in the field.
Fire, black and swift, cleans the meat off bones
and finds the stud's ash, its final form
loosed over a sodden earth; an odor
veils the bright grass as the moist
scent of char holds my breath to the past.
Scared, I retreat to the familiar,
the deaf light of the rabbit, the speed
from his little chalk-covered hands
mimicking movement from where I speak
a voice hidden inside my mouth,
not dark but lusterless, and deep.

6. *Der Erlkönig*

I see you now, lit by my body: evening's
disguise, color of mist, semblance of vines,
the pleach of clouds swollen with hail.
We are touching earth swiftly; you've shown
me how to hide, to escape in flight's shadow.
I see you in the shine of the horse
in hooves moist with alfalfa, slower
in bean-spears and in dirt hay-fragrant.
And I follow through the hands of trees
galloping to accept your gifts, Majesty,
with need to be bells warning of frost.
With love, now, show me how to move.
I have come home to lie down in you—
saintlike and febrile at dusk.

7. To the Body

It is you they want. We have never been
in love. I'm sorry you've had to be cold,
a handful of lice, animal of my heart.
Where have you been? I shall not
look to worry about what you're about
to do to me in the act of omission.
I will no longer contest your being
heavy and always home. Since you're the wanted,
why not give you to their white hand?
Because as I watch, I want you myself.
How awful that we've grown so attached,
that each betrayal brings my fingers back
to you. For tonight, lie with me: I will
be puncture and breath, and you will like that.

8. That the Night Please Us

That's when I woke into the dark white owls,
in medicine. I had become alone.
It was the time before I finished dying,
before I looked for fever in rain,
an illness I could give permission.
Alive in the shaded world of men,
I knew you as pain, as specific need,
as the cold thing that was foreign.
I will always misunderstand the omen,
the obvious image laced in the mind:
all of the life I was not forgetting.
Few appearances are like this. That is why,
ill-lit, I ache as you enter my throat,
rising, a sound in the crowd of the dark.

9. *Ich will ein Reiter werden*

The more you see, the more you will return
to me, where nothing is a memory,
where we remember this the same. I am
place: no secret hearth, no oubliette,
just a simple room, a body wrapped
in hood, small light, susurrus and mud.
Hot with fall and shadows on my hair
my hands lumber onto sand, my knees
release the earth, the grotesque
bulging in the throat, the whole world
coming like a color. As poinsettias
darken by daylight, skin turns heavy
under the douse of sun, the lush and hail
of night: black hurrying hooves.

Nick Norwood

A Palace for the Heart

Just after Ludwig II's death the surgeons opened
   below his ribs and removed his heart:
it's now preserved, indeed enshrined, in a silver vase
   "of French design," and said to rest
in Altötting's Votive Chapel, watched over by
   the "famous miraculous" Black Madonna;
and, perversely curious reading this, I soon pass over
   the question of *why* and turn instead
to wondering *how* exactly his heart resides in there:
   did they leave it simply to slip and slump
into some slouched position? Or is it mounted
   somehow? Propped up? Is it enthroned?
Also, are the hearts of royalty pre-drained? Or
   does the fluid pool, congeal, dry up,
in the bottom's basin? Ridiculous really, when you see
   the big picture: a man reclining
in suburbia, pondering the fate of an inner organ
   long stopped, a continent away,
(not his anyway) absolutely enthralled, engrossed,
   in need of more than blocks on blocks
in La-La Land. Outside, for miles, partitioned lawns
   and sculptured hedges shout out loud,
"We're the bourgeoisie!" But a wretched regiphile
   like me just keeps on sinking, couched
in bloated biographies, revealing all but what
   one wants to know. But, oh, all right,
let's hear it all about the King's alleged fling
   with Richard Wagner, nationalism,
insanity; but, please, get on with it! And on
   to something *edifying*. Yes,

get to the heart of Ludwig's matter: residency.
　Let's glimpse his life in Linderhof:
evenings afloat in his tiny solo shell-shaped boat
　(the lake alit by electric lights!)
in the man-made grotto. Of storm-dense afternoons
　a thorough study ought to explain
how the King climbed Neuschwanstein's tower to watch
　the way rivers into real lakes drain,
alone perhaps, but *gemütlich* and alpinely amused;
　or isolate on an island in
an inland lake in the Louis Schloss, Herrenchiemsee,
　that graceful palace of French design—
as I envision the scene: the King has quietly slipped
　out through the secret-passage door
from his dressing room to the place he most likes to be,
　at ease in a cordate-back settee,
a lounging figure swathed in silk, content to drown
　in cushions stuffed with eiderdown.

Diann Blakely

The Dolls

Those lolling china heads and rag-stuffed arms
will never love us in return, said Rilke,
whose mother dressed him like a girl, whose charms

were sealed in letters for his distant harem.
"How dreadful," he wrote, "to spin our first silk"
for lolling china heads, for rag-stuffed arms

as plump as mine when young: the rich aroma
of cakes rising, cream rising in whole milk.
My mother dressed me like a girl who'd charm

her grownup friends at teas, stroll through museums
and fall in love with statues, like Rilke,
those lolling china heads and rag-stuffed arms

turned to marble Apollos in his poems:
"change your life." Easy for a god to talk—
no mother dressed him like a girl whose charms

were pink and minor, who blinked with alarm
whenever boys asked if she loved them back.
O lolling china heads and rag-stuffed arms!—
still I undressed, a girl with other charms.

A Treatise on Desire

Norman Lock

Mrs. Willoughby woke, because of an insinuating pressure on her thigh. Hearing her stir on the other side of the thin wall that separated her room from mine, I went to her. "My sleep was disturbed," she said. "By someone who entered through the French windows without invitation and stood—there, at the foot of the bed. He stood a long time, watching me sleep, with his hand clutching my thigh. Don't ask me how I know."

"Perhaps you dreamed it," I suggested.

She lifted her nightdress so that I might regard five small bruises on an otherwise immaculate leg.

I regarded them gladly.

"One doesn't expect a nightmare mauling to leave marks!" she replied tartly.

"Was any further harm done you?" I asked, turning away to conceal my anxiety.

She was silent a moment, taking stock. Out in Kilindini Harbor, a hippo snorted. A hyena laughed somewhere in the night. She shook her head and sighed, "It is always so when Mr. Willoughby is out seeing to his affairs."

Mr. Willoughby managed the Uganda railroad. I considered placing my hand on Mrs. Willoughby's thigh in his absence, but didn't.

"And what of Lenin?" I asked instead.

She regarded her bruises, then said, "It has been weeks since I've had him in my bed."

I cleared my throat meaningfully.

"Oh, Vlady is a very nice lover," she continued, "but too serious. He's death at a dinner party."

She sniffed the midnight air, delicately, through her finely shaped nose. I did, too, though mine is not nearly so handsome.

"There!" she said. "Underneath the gladiola—can you smell it?"

I smelled nothing.

"A pungency," she said, sniffing once more. "It is always so after I have been alone a while in bed: the pressure of a hand sufficient to wake me, the bruises, and a pungency underneath the gladiola."

In sympathy I put my hand on hers. In sympathy for her bruises the blood came out on my cheeks and my loins congested.

Heavy footsteps sounded on the veranda. I turned in time to see a shadow shamble into the topiary, to be swallowed by the greater darkness of a moonless night.

Mrs. Willoughby leaned over the marmalade dish.

"Will you stay the night with me?" she asked.

My heart jumped inside my safari jacket.

"Of course, delicious lady!"

"You misunderstand," she said in a tone of unmistakable reproof. "I want you to *watch*."

"Watch?"

(Was Lenin about to take up unlawful residence under Mrs.

Willoughby's mosquito net once again while Mr. Willoughby tended to his railroad?)
"To see what visits me in the night."
My heart sank.
She dabbed my mustache with a napkin to rid it of a crumb of toast. Her *eau de cologne* lingered in the breathless Mombasa morning.
"Come; I want to show you something."
She took me lightly by the arm and guided me into the topiary. Beside the carefully clipped thornbushes taught to grow up outside her bedroom (ah, Beauty!), she pointed out the trampled grass and—in earth still impressionable after the recently ended rains—two enormous footprints that could only be characterized as simian.

I didn't know it at the time, but the footsteps trodden into the rain-sodden earth outside Mrs. Willoughby's bedroom had been left there by Prince Kong. (The same Kong who, as King, would ravish a jodhpured Fay Wray in the 1930s. In 1910, however, he was a moody young gorilla with as yet no appetite for virgin sacrifice.) He had left the family's hereditary stomping grounds in Central Africa and, after a long and circuitous peregrination, found himself in Mrs. Willoughby's topiary garden on the outskirts of Mombasa. At the time, many people were helplessly tramping the length and breadth of the continent, transfixed by the walking sickness that then held sway. To my knowledge, however, no instances of animal contraction of the mysterious malady have ever been verified. Kong, as I would later discover, had been drawn to the open French windows by the strength of Mrs. Willoughby's desire.

August 1910
Mombasa

Dear Siggy,

An interesting case has lately fallen into my lap. A friend is being visited by an ape. She claims "it is always so" when she sleeps alone for any length of time. I would be interested in your analysis. Will you come?

Regards,

N.

September 1910
Zurich

Dear N.,

Visitation by apes is well documented in the literature. The explanation lies in the unconscious: more precisely in the id. Sexual deprivation is, quite obviously, at the root here. The ape is a figment of your friend's overactive imagination. (The ape appears frequently in medieval art as an emblem of licentiousness.)

I am unable to come to Africa and suggest you take matters into your own hand. ("Fallen into my lap"—a revealing Freudian slip—indicates that you may have already done so.)

Yours truly,

Sigmund

P.S. Please do not call me "Siggy."

October 1910
Mombasa

Dear Siggy,

The ape is no figment! I can send you footprints to prove it!

Sincerely,

N.

A TREATISE ON DESIRE

October 1910
Zurich

N.:

You are clearly hysterical and delusional. Keep your footprints, and do not call me "Siggy"!!!

Sigmund Freud

I lay under Mrs. Willoughby's bed and waited. Up above me, Mrs. Willoughby slept, breathing in a way that reminded me of soft, fluttering things: of moths, or a satin camisole dropped negligently over a chair, handled by a wind from an open sash. The jungle came a little way inside the room through the French windows thrown open to receive the balm of night. I listened to it register its agitations and alarms. Later, the moon rose above the topiary and threw the prickly shadow of the thornbushes onto the parquet, which was hard beneath my head.

Soon I, too, was sleeping.

I dreamed that Mrs. Willoughby was carried outside in the hairy arms of Kong (although I did not know his name at the time) into the moonlit topiary. There, on the wrought-iron garden bench, he made love to her: "Sweet Mrs. Willoughby."

"What do you want, you big gorilla?"

"Deep in the Congo, I caught the night-bloom of your desire. I came here to stand by your bed and watch you sleep." He sighed. "I am smitten."

Then with ardor did Kong press Mrs. Willoughby to him. With ardor and with strength of arm. But she repulsed him.

"I'm not attracted to you physically."

He beat his breast. "I can give you what no man can!"

(Leering braggadocio!)

"But I like men," she said.

"If you sleep with me, Beauty, there's every possibility that I might change into a man. I'm already a prince."

"I have a lover as well as a husband who, though seldom home, adds a certain *frisson* to my extramarital affairs."

Does she mean me? I wondered. Does she consider me her lover? We had twice or thrice dallied playfully under the mosquito net; but each time I had come away feeling that I had failed to measure up. Perhaps she means Lenin. Vladimir Ilyich might not possess charm, such as one values in a dinner guest or pinochle partner; but he has charisma in spite of his unstylish clothes and muddy shoes. Charisma in abundance, else how could he, seven years hence, foment a revolution of such magnitude as to topple the Romanovs' centuries-old rule?

The coming war would do much, of course, to weaken the monarchic hold on Russia. (Have I not told you how it was to weaken reason's hold—not only on nation-states but on my own state of mind—how *nervous* that war would make me, nervous as I was—am—have always been—my whole life long? Perhaps I have not yet told you, but that war, the so-called Great War, did considerable damage to my *sangfroid*.

"*Chérie*," said Kong, fiddling with Mrs. Willoughby's nightdress.

Mrs. Willoughby slapped the brute.

Kong wept, inconsolable.

I woke in Mrs. Willoughby's bed to find myself fiddling with her nightdress, with the buttons that did up the front. She was furious. "You have betrayed my trust!" she said. "You've played the brute as surely as that hairy ape did." I remarked that, unlike the hairy ape, I had not bruised her; but she took no notice. "Leave me at once!" she commanded, giving me a shove. I fell out of bed.

"I was dreaming!" I protested in mitigation. "One isn't responsible for acts committed while asleep."

I sat in the library, admiring Mr. Willoughby's collection of Victorian erotica and a magnificent Cornwallis Harris portfolio of rhinoceros engravings. I also admired Mr. Willoughby's Bombay gin; and my admiration, though not unbounded, was sufficient to drain the neck of a recently unstoppered bottle.

Mr. Willoughby's man knocked softly at the door before entering with a silver tray. He coughed discreetly into his fist, then, inclining towards me so that his black swallowtail opened gracefully, indicated a gilt-edged calling card.

I took the card from the tray and read: "Prince Ali Kong. The Congo."

"Shall I show the gentleman in?" Mr. Willoughby's man asked.

"I don't wish to see him," I said disdainfully.

"If you'll pardon me, sir—the gentleman insists."

"Tell Kong I am not at home!" I shouted. "Tell him that I do not talk to primates!"

"Very good, sir."

Mr. Willoughby's man nodded and left the library.

I folded my hands on the fumed-oak desk (not in prayer, but in perplexity) and pondered the curious geometry in which I seemed to have become suddenly enmeshed. And then, astonished, I looked towards the library casement: someone was outside, scratching at the window!

The following exchange occurred through the open window. To tell the truth, I was afraid to meet Kong otherwise. Gorillas, no matter how polished their manner, retain a dark and brutal instinct. Which is only natural. While Kong may have distinguished himself among beasts, he was one after all; his top hat, spats, gloves and fastidious grooming did not for a moment make me forget his origins. (As a convinced Darwinian, I recognized in Kong a tenuous propinquity; but as a man, on safari in Africa, I was unwilling to accord him anything like equal status. While not one to lord it over the beasts, I nevertheless relished my superior evolution.)

"You refused to see me," said Kong, offended.

"Yes."

"Why?"

"We can have nothing to say to each other."

I looked away, unable to meet his piercing gaze.

"I disagree," he said. "There's Mrs. Willoughby."

"What about Mrs. Willoughby?" I bristled, not liking her name in his mouth.

"It seems we are both in love with her," said Kong with admirable simplicity.

I disguised my admiration with a rebuke: "Whether I am or not is none of your concern! You, on the other hand, have no business loving her!" Indignant, I began to close the window but was prevented by his large hand and muscular arm.

"Because we are of different races?" he demanded, and beneath the demand I detected the grievance of the perpetually slighted.

"Because we are of different species!" I snarled.

He kept silent a moment before continuing evenly: "Either you leave the field to me, or you will meet me on the field of honor."

Mrs. Willoughby was sleeping. I shook her—gently, then roughly—but she would not wake. Apparently she had contracted the sleeping sickness, which, like the walking sickness, was then general throughout Africa. She might sleep for weeks—or months—before waking. I undid her buttons and undressed her. I considered whether or not to make love to her while she slept but decided against it. To my mind it smacked of necrophilia—a practice I detested. I did, however, study her nakedness. It was pink and round and fragrant. It was the nakedness of a woman in the prime of life, and I longed to embrace it. But I continued in my resolve not to interfere with her sleeping.

I bit my lip and sighed, "Oh, Mrs. Willoughby!"

I prayed that she might wake, that I might gather her to me; but she did not wake.

I sat by the bed on a rattan chair and kept watch as I had promised her. Kong is here because she sleeps, I reasoned. He is no delusion or manifestation of hysteria, but a very real presence unleashed by Mrs. Willoughby's dreams. Neither nightmare nor incubus, but *substance* (even if hirsute). A

A TREATISE ON DESIRE

pulse of erotic energy—embodied and clothed. Kong would be detained in Mombasa, in the vicinity of Mrs. Willoughby, who would be helpless before his depredations for as long as she slept. (I had no faith in Kong's self-restraint or finer feelings, given the bruises imprinted on her thigh.)

"Oh, wake up, Mrs. Willoughby! Wake!" I shouted.

She was far down in the depths of sleep. I would have needed a grappling hook to raise her.

Night fell and the shadow of the thorns invaded the room. A wind flooded through the French windows and with it a pungency underneath the scent of gladiola.

"I think you do not understand desire," said Kong.

I looked at the sleeping Mrs. Willoughby and assured him I did.

"I don't mean the sudden arousals of your kind that are just as suddenly quelled; I mean desire as a paroxysm of nature. Violent biological upheaval. Wildfire sweeping the blood. A glandular storm wracking body and nerves. Savagery and exaltation unknown in New York, London, or Paris."

He took off his hat and coat, spats and lemon-colored gloves, his shirt and trousers. He stripped to his essence—the elemental condition of his kind. I saw strength of will revealed in a purely physical nature—vitality that transcended brutishness. He grew before my eyes, and in spite of myself I envied him. Then just as quickly as he had divested himself of the trappings of civilization, he put them on again and resumed the stature of a man.

"Where I come from," he said, "all is desire; all life comes into being by its force; all is copulation and increase. All is—if you will pardon me—the long, tireless fuck of creation." Kong stroked the sleeping woman's thigh; she stirred in her sleep and smiled. "She knows," he said; "as long as she dreams, she knows desire's force."

Fury rose up in me—fury that Mrs. Willoughby should be used so. I pulled his hand roughly away.

He slapped my face with a lemon-colored glove.

"Cigars at dawn," he said.

Siggy, Siggy—how I wish you were here! To be challenged by an ape in spats and yellow gloves to a duel with *cigars*! How absurd! How Freudian! And how does one fight a duel with cigars?

We met in the summerhouse behind the topiary. We faced each other across a pinochle table. Mr. Willoughby's man entered with a mahogany humidor, which he placed on the green baize. On a distant lawn a badminton game was in progress. I listened to the shuttlecock strumming the racquets. Who can be playing badminton at this hour? I wondered as Kong selected a cigar.
"Partagas," he said, sniffing it with the air of a connoisseur.
"One of Mr. Willoughby's favorites," his man said approvingly.
I chose a democratic Virginian with a Connecticut wrapper.
Mr. Willoughby's man clipped the ends in a miniature guillotine and, having returned them to us, lit them.
"Close the windows, then leave us," said Kong with a peremptory wave of his cigar's burning end.
The man left, shutting the door behind him.
We sat in silence, the heavy blue smoke tumbling in the light that fell through the closed summerhouse windows. Eyes watering, throat burning, I thought of Mrs. Willoughby asleep in her bedroom and wondered if she was worth it. Ashamed, I sucked vigorously at my cigar, expelling clouds of pungent smoke across the pinochle table. Kong was unperturbed.
The pungency! I said to myself. The pungency underneath the gladiola!
It was then I lost consciousness.

We seemed to make love under water. The air wavered, the light shook down over us. Mrs. Willoughby drifted, her long auburn hair floating like weed. I swam above her attentively, darting here and there to give her what pleasure I could. Had I spoken, I would have told her how I desired her; but I did not speak. Because of the water, because I had no wish to drown in the act of love, nor of speech either. I looked up at last and saw Kong, his broad face smiling in benediction. The end of his cigar extinguished.

I shrugged into consciousness in Mrs. Willoughby's bedroom. By what mysterious mode of locomotion I had arrived there, I cannot say. Mrs. Willoughby was gone. I examined the bed for signs of struggle but could find none.

I went out to the summerhouse in search of Kong; but he, too, seemed to have vanished without leaving so much as a cigar ash to signify his presence. The gladiola were in full force, scenting the clear Mombasa morning. The shadows of the thornbushes were rolling back towards the topiary as the sun advanced. Birdsong replaced that of the shuttlecock.

I found Mr. Willoughby's man in the conservatory, polishing the horn of the gramophone. Recordings of Brahms's four symphonies were stacked on a taboret. Mrs. Willoughby believed that plant life flourished in the presence of soothing melody. For this, she was derided as a crackpot. (I had no opinion one way or the other, though I had often come to her defense in the Mombasa Hotel Bar, in order to insinuate myself into her favor.)

"Have you seen Mrs. Willoughby?" I asked the man.

"Gone, sir," he replied, putting down his chamois cloth.

"Gone?"

"Carried off by the hairy gentleman."

It was as I had feared.

"Where?"

He pointed beyond the topiary to a darkness. An obscurity. A silence punctuated by strange cries. "The jungle, sir." He handed me a book bound in soft leather: *A Treatise on Desire* by A. Kong. "He said I was to give you this."

I opened the book and began to read: "*Desire begins in sleep....*"

NOTES ON CONTRIBUTORS

FICTION

Louis de Bernières has worked as a teacher, a cowboy, a mechanic and a landscape gardener. He is the author of a trilogy of tragicomic novels, including *Corelli's Mandolin*. His most recent novel is *The Troublesome Offspring of Cardinal Guzman*. This story is also published in Great Britain in the November issue of *The Tatler*.

A.L. Kennedy is the author of two collections of short stories and two novels. Her third novel, *Original Bliss*, is forthcoming this winter. She lives in Scotland. This is her first American publication.

Norman Lock's plays have been produced throughout the United States, as well as in Scotland, Germany and Italy. "A Treatise on Desire" is from *A History of the Imagination*, a collection of interrelated stories. He received the 1979 Aga Khan Prize for Fiction for his story "The Love of Stanley Marvel & Claire Moon."

J. David Stevens is an assistant professor of creative writing at Seton Hall University. His most recent microfictions appear or are forthcoming in *The Iowa Review*, *The North American Review*, *The Cream City Review* and *Witness*.

Joy Williams lives in Arizona and Key West. She is the author of six books, the most recent of which is *Escapes*, a collection of stories.

FEATURES

Simon Armitage's collection of essays and autobiographical sketches *All Points North*, from which the feature in this issue is excerpted, was published by Viking U.K. this fall. He has written numerous books of poetry, the most recent of which is *CloudCuckooLand*.

Kurt Vonnegut is the author of fourteen novels, including *Cat's Cradle*, *Slaughterhouse Five* and *Breakfast of Champions*. His most recent novel, published last fall, is *Timequake*.

POETRY

Neil Azevedo's poems have appeared in *Western Humanities Review*, *Raritan Quarterly*, *The Nebraska Review* and *The Notre Dame Review*. He lives with his family in New York City.

Diann Blakely teaches at a girls' prep school in Nashville and assists with the poetry editorship of *The Antioch Review*. Her first book, *Hurricane Walk*, was published in 1992.

Scott Coffel, a graduate of the Iowa Writer's Workshop, has poems forthcoming in a number of magazines, including *The American Scholar* and *The Wallace Stevens Journal*.

Alfred Corn published his seventh volume of poems, *Present*, last year, as well as his first novel, *Part of His Story*. His collected poems are due to appear in the fall of 1999 under the title *Stake: Poems, 1972–1992*.

Rachel Hadas's most recent collection is *Halfway Down the Hall: New and Selected Poems*.

Anthony Hecht's most recent publication is *The Gehenna Florilegium*, which includes woodcuts by Leonard Baskin.

Melanie Hope works at Poet's House in New York City.

Sue Kwock Kim's poems have appeared in *The New Republic*, *Poetry*, *The Nation* and a number of other journals. She is currently a Fulbright Fellow in Korea.

Wayne Koestenbaum's third collection of poetry, *The Milk of Inquiry*, will be published by Persea in 1999. He is a professor of English at the Graduate Center of the City University of New York.

Daniel Kunitz is the managing editor of *The Paris Review*.

Richard Lamb is the assistant editor of *The New Leader*.

Rachel Loden's first collection of poems, *The Last Campaign*, will be published this winter.

Stephen McLeod's poems have appeared in *The Paris Review*, *Ploughshares*, *Southwest Review* and *Western Humanities Review*. He is an assistant district attorney for Kings County (Brooklyn) and lives in New York City.

John McKernan teaches at Marshall University. The poems in this issue are part of a chapbook, *Postcard from Dublin*, scheduled for publication next summer.

Susan Mitchell's *Rapture* was a finalist for the National Book Award and winner of the first Kingsley Tufts Poetry Award. Her third book of poetry is forthcoming in 1999.

NOTES ON CONTRIBUTORS

Nick Norwood's work has recently appeared in *Western Humanities Review*. His collection *Laments for Ludwig II* is forthcoming in the James Dickey Contemporary Poetry Series published by the University of South Carolina Press.

Eric Ormsby is the author, most recently, of the collection *For a Modest God: New and Selected Poems*. The poems in this issue are from *Araby*, his forthcoming collection.

Kathleen Peirce's new collection of poems, *The Oval Hour*, will be published this spring. She teaches in the MFA program at Southwest Texas State University. The poems entitled Confessions in this issue derive some language from *The Confessions of St. Augustine* translated by E.B. Pusey.

Carl Phillips is the author of three volumes of poetry, including *From the Devotions* (1998). A recent Guggenheim Fellow, he teaches at Washington University in St. Louis.

Bin Ramke edits the *Denver Quarterly* and a poetry series for the University of Georgia Press. His sixth book of poems, *Wake*, will be published by the University of Iowa Press this spring. He teaches writing and literature at the University of Denver.

Stephen Sandy's most recent book of poems, *The Thread: New and Selected Poems*, was published by Louisiana State University Press. His next collection, *Black Box*, is forthcoming this spring.

Daniel Tobin is the winner of a fellowship from the National Endowment for the Arts. His book of poems, *Where the World Is Made*, won the Bakeless Prize in poetry for 1998.

Kevin Young's first book, *Most Way Home*, won the National Poetry Series and the Vacharis First Book Prize from *Ploughshares*. He is an assistant professor of English and African-American Studies at the University of Georgia.

INTERVIEWS

Jonathan Rosen (V.S. Naipaul interview) is the culture editor of *The Forward*. His novel *Eve's Apple* was published in paperback by Plume earlier this year. His essays have appeared in various publications, including the *New York Times Book Review*, *Vanity Fair* and *The American Scholar*.

Wallace Shawn (Mark Strand interview) has been writing plays for thirty years. Mark Strand played a role in his most recent play, *The Designated Mourner*, when it premiered in 1995. *Four Plays: A Thought in Three Parts, Marie and Bruce, Aunt Dan and Lemon, and The Fever* was published by Farrar, Straus and Giroux in 1998.

Tarun Tejpal (V.S. Naipaul interview) is the editor of the Indian magazine *Outlook*.

NOTES ON CONTRIBUTORS

ART

Karen Kilimnik is represented by 303 Gallery in New York City.
Alan Loehle is represented by the Viridian Gallery in New York City.
Mark Strand is represented by Harlan & Weaver in New York City. He is the subject of an interview in this issue.

STATEMENT required by the act of August 24, 1912 as amended by the acts of March 3, 1933, and July 2, 1946. (Title 39, United States Code, Section 233) showing the ownership, management, and circulation of THE PARIS REVIEW published quarterly at Flushing, New York, 11358.

1. *Editor:* George Plimpton, *Managing Editor:* Daniel Kunitz, 541 East 72 Street, New York, N.Y. *Business Manager:* Lillian Von Nickern, 45-39 171st Place, Flushing, N.Y.

2. The owners are: The Paris Review, Inc., George Plimpton, Peter Matthiessen, Thomas H. Guinzburg. All c/o Plimpton, 541 E. 72 Street, NY, NY 10021.

3. The known bondholders, mortgages, and other security holders owning or holding 1 percent or more of total amounts of bonds, mortgages, or other securities are: None.

4. Paragraphs 2 and 3 include, in cases where the stock holder or security holder appears upon the books of the company as trustee or in any other fiduciary relation, the name of the person or corporation for whom such trustee is acting; also the statements in the two paragraphs show the affiant's full knowledge and belief as to the circumstances and conditions under which the stock holders and security holders who do not appear upon the books of the company as trustees, hold stocks and securities in a capacity other than that of a bona fide owner.

5. Extent and nature of circulation: Average number of copies each issue during preceding 12 months (actual number of copies of single issue published nearest to filing date):

Total/number copies (Average): 10910 (10270) Paid and/or requested circulation (Sales through dealers and carriers, street vendors and counter sales): 6196 (5619) Mail Subscription: 2509 (2630) Free distribution by mail, carrier, or other means, samples, complimentary, and other free copies: 484 (501) Total Distribution: 9189 (8750). Copies not distributed (office use, left over, unaccounted, spoiled after printing): 1721 (960). Copies not distributed (return from news agents): N/A (560) Total: 10910 (10270).

Marjorie Kalman, Notary Public, State of New York —Daniel Kunitz
No. 4955336 Managing Editor
Qualified in New York County
Commission Expires August 28, 1999

The Paris Review Booksellers Advisory Board

THE PARIS REVIEW BOOKSELLERS ADVISORY BOARD is a group of owners and managers of independent bookstores from around the world who have agreed to share with us their knowledge and expertise.

ANDREAS BROWN, *Gotham Bookmart, New York, NY*
CHAPMAN, DRESCHER & PETERSON,
   Bloomsbury Bookstore, Ashland, OR
ROBERT CONTANT, *St. Mark's Bookstore, New York, NY*
JOHN EKLUND, *Harry W. Schwartz Bookshop, Milwaukee, WI*
JOSEPH GABLE, *Borders Bookshop, Ann Arbor, MI*
THOMAS GLADYSZ, *The Booksmith, San Francisco, CA*
HELENE GOLAY, *The Corner Bookstore, New York, NY*
GLEN GOLDMAN, *Booksoup, West Hollywood, CA*
JAMES HARRIS, *Prairie Lights Bookstore, Iowa City, IA*
ODILE HELLIER, *Village Voice, Paris, France*
RICHARD HOWORTH, *Square Books, Oxford, MS*
KARL KILIAN, *Brazos Bookstore, Houston, TX*
KRIS KLEINDIENST, *Left Bank Books, St. Louis, MO*
FRANK KRAMER, *Harvard Bookstore, Cambridge, MA*
RUPERT LECRAW, *Oxford Books, Atlanta, GA*
TERRI MERZ and ROBIN DIENER, *Chapters,
   Washington, DC*
MICHAEL POWELL, *Powell's Bookstore, Portland, OR*
DONALD PRETARI, *Black Oak Books, Berkeley, CA*
JACQUES RIEUX, *Stone Lion Bookstore, Fort Collins, CO*
ANDREW ROSS, *Cody's, Berkeley, CA*
HENRY SCHWAB, *Bookhaven, New Haven, CT*
RICK SIMONSON, *Eliot Bay, Seattle, WA*
LOUISA SOLANO, *Grolier Bookshop, Cambridge, MA*
JIM TENNEY, *Olsson's Books, Washington, D.C.*
DAVID UNOWSKY, *Hungry Mind Bookstore, St. Paul, MN*
JOHN VALENTINE, *Regulator Bookshop, Durham, NC*

Available now from the Flushing office
BACK ISSUES OF THE PARIS REVIEW

No.		
18	Ernest Hemingway Interview; Giacometti Portfolio; Philip Roth Fiction.	$25.00
25	Robert Lowell Interview; Hughes Rudd, X.J. Kennedy.	10.00
30	S.J. Perelman and Evelyn Waugh Interviews; Niccolo Tucci, 22 poets.	10.00
35	William Burroughs Interview; Irvin Faust, Leonard Gardner, Ron Padgett.	10.00
37	Allen Ginsberg and Cendrars Interviews; Charles Olson, Gary Snyder.	10.00
44	Creeley and I.B. Singer Interviews; James Salter, Diane di Prima.	15.00
45	Updike Interview; Hoagland Journal; Veitch, Brautigan, Padgett, O'Hara.	10.00
46	John Dos Passos Interview; Thomas M. Disch, Ted Berrigan, Kenneth Koch.	10.00
47	Robert Graves Interview; Ed Sanders, Robert Creeley, Tom Clark.	10.00
62	James Wright Interview; Joe Brainard, Christo Portfolio.	10.00
63	J.P. Donleavy and Steinbeck Interviews; Louis Simpson, Robert Bly.	10.00
64	Kingsley Amis and P.G. Wodehouse Interviews; Diane Vreuls, Thomas M. Disch.	10.00
66	Stanley Elkin Interview; Richard Stern, W.S. Merwin.	10.00
67	Cheever and Wheelock Interviews; Maxine Kumin, Aram Saroyan.	10.00
68	William Goyen Interview; John Updike, William Stafford.	10.00
69	Kurt Vonnegut Interview; William Burroughs, Ed Sanders, John Logan.	10.00
70	William Gass Interview; Peter Handke, William S. Wilson, Galway Kinnell.	10.00
72	Richard Wilbur Interview; Joy Williams, Norman Dubie.	10.00
73	James M. Cain and Anthony Powell Interviews; Dallas Wiebe, Bart Midwood.	10.00
74	Didion, Drabble and Oates Interviews; Vincente Aleixandre Portfolio; Max Apple.	10.00
75	Gardner, Shaw Interviews; Handke Journal, Dubus, Salter, Gunn, Heaney.	10.00
76	Ignatow, Levi, Rhys Interviews; Jean Rhys Memoir Louis Simpson.	10.00
77	Stephen Spender Interview; Mark Strand, Joseph Brodsky, Philip Levine.	10.00
78	Andrei Voznesensky Interview; Voznesensky/Ginsberg Conversation; Edie Sedgwick Memoir; T. Coraghessan Boyle, Tom Disch, Odysseus Elytis.	15.00
79	25th ANNIVERSARY: R. West Interview; Paris Review Sketchbook; Hemingway, Faulkner, Southern, Gass, Carver, Dickey, Schuyler, Gellhorn/Spender/Jackson Letters.	15.00
80	Barthelme, Bishop Interviews; Reinaldo Arenas, J.D. Salinger Feature.	10.00
81	T. Williams, P. Bowles Interviews; Wiebe, Atwood, Federman Fiction; Montale Poetry.	20.00
83	J. Brodsky, S. Kunitz Interviews; Gerald Stern/B.F. Conners Prize Poetry.	15.00
84	P. Larkin, J. Merrill Interviews; T.C. Boyle, Edmund White Fiction.	15.00
85	M. Cowley, W. Maxwell Interviews; H. Brodkey, Bill Knott Poetry.	15.00
87	H. Boll, Infante Interviews; Milosz, C.K. Williams Poetry.	10.00
88	Gordimer, Carver Interviews; Hill, Nemerov Poetry; McCourt, Davis Fiction.	10.00
89	James Laughlin, May Sarton Interviews; F. Bidart Poetry, Zelda Fitzgerald Feature.	10.00
90	John Ashbery, James Laughlin Interviews; C. Wright Poetry; E. Garber Fiction.	10.00
91	J Baldwin, E. Wiesel Interviews; Morand, R. Wilson Fiction; Clampitt Poetry.	10.00
92	M. Kundera, E. O'Brien, A. Koestler Interviews; E.L. Doctorow Fiction.	10.00
93	30th ANNIV: Roth, Ionesco, Cortazar Interviews; Rush, Boyle Fiction; Brodsky, Carver Poetry.	15.00
97	Hollander, McGuane Interviews; Dickey, Kosinski Features; Dixon Fiction, Wright Poetry.	15.00
98	L. Edel, R. Stone Interviews; R. Stone Fiction; L. Edel Feature.	10.00
99	A. Robbe-Grillet, K. Shapiro Interviews; E. Tallent Fiction; D. Hall Poetry.	10.00
100	DOUBLE 100th: Hersey, Irving Interviews; Gordimer, Munro Fiction; Merrill, Milosz Poetry.	15.00
105	Calisher, Gaddis Interviews; B. Okri Fiction; A. Zagajewski Poetry.	15.00
106	35th ANNIV: Lessing, Yourcenar Interviews; C. Smith Fiction; Logue Poetry; Styron Feature.	15.00
108	A. Hecht, E. White Interviews; C. Baxter, J. Kauffman Fiction; S. Olds Poetry.	10.00
109	Mortimer, Stoppard Interviews; Burroughs, Minot Fiction; Mathews, Simic Poetry.	10.00
111	Fowles, Fugard, Spencer Interviews; Tucci, Gurganus Fiction; Proust, Rilke Translations.	10.00
112	Kennedy, Skvorecky Interviews; Malamud, Maspéro Fiction; Perec, Pinsky Poetry.	10.00
114	Sarraute, Settle Interviews; Matthiessen, P. West Fiction; F. Wright Poetry.	10.00
115	Murdoch, Stegner Interviews; Bass Fiction; Laughlin Poetry; Merwin Feature.	10.00
116	Angelou, Vargas Llosa Interviews; Perec Fiction; Ashbery Poetry; Stein Feature.	10.00
117	Atwood, Pritchett Interviews; R. Price, Stern Fiction; Kizer, Logue Poetry.	10.00
118	Bloom, Wolfe Interviews; Tolstaya Fiction; Ashbery Poetry; Carver, Burgess Features.	10.00
119	Grass, Paz Interviews; M. McCarthy Feature; DeMarinis Fiction; Bonnefoy, Hacker Poetry.	10.00
120	Hall, Morris Interviews; Milosz Feature; Brodkey, Mailer Fiction; Corn, Lasdun Poetry.	10.00
121	Brodkey, Price Interviews; Minot, West Fiction; Z. Herbert Poetry; D. Hall Feature.	10.00
122	Amichai, Simon Interviews; Konrád Fiction; Montale, Zarin Poetry; Merrill Feature.	10.00
123	Mahfouz Interview; J. Scott Fiction; Ashbery, Sarton Poetry; Schwartz-Laughlin Letters.	10.00
124	Calvino, Paley Interviews; Grass, Johnson, Moore Fiction; Clampitt, Herbert Poetry.	10.00
126	Clampitt, Helprin Interviews; J. Williams, Eco Fiction; Goldbarth, Zarin Poetry.	10.00
127	Logue, Salter Interviews; Carroll, Shepard Fiction; Ammons, Swenson Poetry.	10.00
128	40th ANNIV: DeLillo, Morrison Interviews; Canin, García Márquez Fiction; Graham, Merwin Poetry; Cheever, Hemingway, Pound Documents.	15.00
129	Stafford Interview; J. Scott Fiction; Yenser Poetry; Salter, Trilling Features.	10.00
130	Kesey, Snodgrass Interviews; Braverman, Power Fiction; Paz Poetry.	10.00
131	Bonnefoy, Munro Interviews; Moody, Pritchard Fiction; Hacker, Merrill Poetry; Bishop-Swenson Letters.	10.00
132	Auchincloss, Gottlieb Interviews; Gass, Thon, West Fiction; Kinnell Poetry, Kazin Feature.	10.00
133	Achebe, Milosz Interviews; Byatt, D'Ambrosio Fiction; Hirsch, Wagoner Poetry.	10.00
134	Hughes, Levi Interviews; Fischer, Schulman Fiction; Ammons, Kizer Poetry; Welty Feature.	10.00
135	Gunn, P.D. James, O'Brian Interviews; DeMarinis, Mayo, Prose Fiction; Rich, Wright Poetry.	10.00
136	HUMOR: Allen, Keillor, Trillin Interviews; Barth, Boyle Fiction; Clifton, Updike Poetry; Bloom Feature.	30.00
137	Sontag, Steiner Interviews; Bass Fiction; Seshadri Poetry; Russian Feature.	10.00
138	SCREENWRITING: Dunne, Price, Wilder Interviews; Diaz Fiction; Southern Feature.	10.00
139	Ammons, Buckley, Cela Interviews; Davenport, Franzen Fiction; Kizer Poetry.	10.00
140	Ford, Oz Interviews; Butler, Eakins Fiction; Bidart, Olds Poetry; Cooper Feature.	10.00
141	Snyder, Vendler Interviews; New Fiction; New Poetry; Marquez Feature.	10.00
142	THEATER: Mamet, Shepard, Wasserstein Interviews; McDonagh Play.	15.00
143	Le Carré, Morris Interviews; Oates, Powell, Smith Fiction; Merwin Poetry; Salter Feature.	10.00
144	Heaney, Pinsky Interviews; Moody, Wallace Fiction; Hacker, Szymborska Poetry.	10.00
145	Rosset, Winterson Interviews; Millhauser, Richard Fiction; Hirsch Poetry.	10.00
146	BRITAIN: Amis Interview; Byatt, Foden, Self Fiction; Armitage, Motion Poetry.	10.00
147	Banks, Kadaré Interviews; Bass, Cooley, Knight Fiction; An Oulipo Sampler.	10.00

Please add $3.00 for postage and handling for up to 2 issues; $4.75 for 3 to 5. Payment should accompany order. For orders outside the U.S. please double the shipping costs. Payments must be made in U.S. currency. Prices and availability subject to change. Address orders to: 45-39 171 Place, Flushing, N.Y. 11358

MASTERCARD/VISA # _____ EXP. DATE _____

The Paris Review mourns the death last autumn of Dr. Charles Attwood. He was a fond friend and supporter of the magazine. He gave annually to a fund to assist the financial needs of the magazine's interns and readers. A manner of his commitment to the Review is suggested by his family's wish prior to the memorial service that donations in lieu of flowers should be sent to the fund to benefit what he considered one of his favorite charities. His friendship and dedication to the magazine will be sorely missed.